Taking Charge

Taking Charge

A School-Based Life Skills Program for Adolescent Mothers

Mary Beth Harris and Cynthia Franklin

OXFORD
UNIVERSITY PRESS
2008

OXFORD
UNIVERSITY PRESS

Oxford University Press, Inc., publishes works that further
Oxford University's objective of excellence
in research, scholarship, and education.

Oxford   New York
Auckland   Cape Town   Dar es Salaam   Hong Kong   Karachi
Kuala Lumpur   Madrid   Melbourne   Mexico City   Nairobi
New Delhi   Shanghai   Taipei   Toronto

With offices in
Argentina   Austria   Brazil   Chile   Czech Republic   France   Greece
Guatemala   Hungary   Italy   Japan   Poland   Portugal   Singapore
South Korea   Switzerland   Thailand   Turkey   Ukraine   Vietnam

Published by Oxford University Press, Inc.
198 Madison Avenue, New York, New York 10016

www.oup.com

Oxford is a registered trademark of Oxford University Press

Library of Congress Cataloging-in-Publication Data
Harris, Mary Beth.
Taking charge : a school-based life skills program for adolescent mothers /
Mary Beth Harris and Cynthia Franklin.
p. cm.
Includes bibliographical references.
ISBN 978-0-19-517294-2 (pbk.)
1. Pregnant schoolgirls—Education—United States.   2. Teenage mothers—
Education—United States.   3. Dropouts—United States.   4. Teenage
mothers—United States—Life skills guides.   I. Franklin, Cynthia.   II. Title.
LC4091.H36 2007
371.93086'5—dc22   2007003035

1 3 5 7 9 8 6 4 2
Printed in the United States of America
on acid-free paper

Preface

Family life and health education teachers and other school-support professionals—such as school social workers, counselors, nurses, and psychologists who work with pregnant and parenting students on a daily basis—know that adolescent pregnancy is a present and daunting social problem challenging public schools across the country. Although the United States has seen a steady decline in teen births since the early 1990s, the country still has the highest adolescent birth rate of any industrialized nation in the world. At some point, most adolescent mothers are students in public schools, and it is to the advantage of the mothers, their children, and society if young mothers continue to progress in school. Recent policy changes restricting economic subsidies and special programs for mothers and children demand that these mothers become self-sufficient and quickly achieve economic and social stability for their young families. More than ever, these young women must have an educational background that prepares them to be their own productive wage earners. Finishing their education is the first critical step and the major building block for both mother and child.

Policy changes also make it necessary, more than ever, for public schools to effectively educate all students, including those who are pregnant and parenting. This is a compelling task for education professionals because adolescent pregnancy is one of the main reasons young women leave school prematurely. For this reason, it is very important for school professionals to have effective curriculums and programs that can assure the success of pregnant and parenting adolescents in public schools.

The purpose of this book is to provide a step-by-step leadership, training, and practice guide for the Taking Charge group curriculum so that school professionals can effectively make use of the curriculum with adolescent mothers. School achievement and positive life outcomes for pregnant and parenting adolescents were our first and foremost goals for the Taking Charge group curriculum. As developers of this curriculum, we have a deep conviction that comes from our personal experiences and clinical work with adolescents. This conviction led us to create a curriculum with the purpose of empowering young women to achieve despite their circumstances of early motherhood. Call us optimistic if you will, but with this curriculum we choose to have faith in young women and the resilience of the human spirit. We believe that becoming an adolescent mother need not be a reason to drop out of school, and neither does having a child in the teenage years have to force a young woman to give up on her academic achievement or her future. We are not naïve, and we know that the choices to bear children in the adolescent years are not easy ones to live through. This life path is certainly not preferable for school and career goals, but once a young woman chooses to raise a child, her destiny is forever intertwined with parenthood.

Despite these facts, we have found that awfulizing over the consequences of having a baby at 15 or 16 does not lead to productive outcomes for young women. We developed the Taking Charge group curriculum so that school professionals can help young women transcend these personal circumstances. Contrary to the mainstream idea that once a teenager gives birth to one or more children, she is doomed, the Taking Charge group curriculum provides the knowledge and skills needed to help young women stay in school and work through the life issues essential to building a promising future.

The Taking Charge curriculum also gives young adolescent mothers a very different message about their future from what they may encounter in society. The message embedded in the curriculum is one of self-efficacy and self-confidence—I can and will persist until I succeed, even though I am a teenage mom. The curriculum builds on a young woman's strengths and uses an empowerment approach. We believe that young mothers need a solid faith in their strengths and in their potential to overcome adversities, enhanced with active social problem-solving and coping skills that enable them to manage the challenges of school, personal relationships, parenting, and employment/career.

Contents of This Book

We developed the Taking Charge group curriculum to be a strengths-based approach to adolescent motherhood, using the best evidence-based research that we could find to construct it. We discuss this development in more detail in chapters 1 and 2, including the theoretical background of the approach. In brief, what we constructed, based on the research literature, is an 8-session goal-oriented, task-centered group program. It is grounded in social learning and cognitive-behavioral theories with a developmental and solution-focused framework that builds on strengths and resources.

Cognitive-behavioral curriculums that address skills training for school completion have found their way into effective models with a number of adolescent groups vulnerable to school dropout (e.g., Dupper, 1998; Forman, Linney, & Brondino, 1990). Few such curriculums, however, have specifically addressed the skills and life issues of adolescent mothers. The Taking Charge curriculum focuses particular emphasis on the mothers graduating from high school, because school dropout is alarmingly high with adolescent mothers and is strongly associated with long-term unemployment and poverty. The focus on school achievement makes the Taking Charge group curriculum especially suited for use in schools.

Chapter 3 presents a practice manual that serves as a step-by-step guide for use in schools, along with the needed forms and materials. It is complete with examples and training materials needed to conduct each session of the group curriculum. Chapters 4 and 5 are provided as complements to chapter 3. Chapter 4 provides detailed information on how to lead successful groups, as well as specific guidance for carrying out activities within the Taking Charge group. It contains case examples of specific procedures required to conduct the group, along with case examples and information on how to be an effective instructor with the curriculum.

Chapter 5 focuses on culturally competent group leadership, using practical examples to demonstrate skills needed to engage culturally diverse student groups. The original Taking Charge group curriculum was designed for work with immigrant and Mexican American students, and the curriculum was found to be effective with that population. Since that time, we have used the curriculum effectively with African American, European American, and some Asian students. In each instance, we have observed that the curriculum is applicable to diverse student populations.

We believe, however, that the curriculum provides the most advantages for culturally diverse and immigrant students because these students also have the highest incidence of adolescent pregnancy and dropout and are growing in numbers in American schools. The U.S. Department of Education, Institute of Educational Sciences reports, for example, that in 2004 Hispanics accounted for 25% of the status dropout rate (students ages 16–24 who were out of school without high school credential) and Hispanics born outside the United states (immigrants) accounted for a whopping 38% of the status dropout rate that year (cited in the National Center for Education Statistics, 2006). Schools are increasingly held accountable for educating all students and the consequences for not being able to effectively do so are important to all society. School professionals may find that Taking Charge is a welcome program to have in hand for growing Hispanic and immigrant populations because our experience with the curriculum has repeatedly suggested that culturally diverse students respond favorably to the program. The Taking Charge curriculum provides a needed resource that can help school professionals span the boundaries of social class, race, and culture with adolescent mothers.

Once we developed the curriculum, we started the long journey to complete outcome research on the curriculum in school settings, to see whether the curriculum was helpful to the pregnant and parenting adolescent women in the groups in which we were able to test it. Actually, we were testing our larger assumption that these young women could be resilient and that they could improve their attendance and grades in school and other critical skills needed to navigate their lives. We were convinced that, even with a baby in arms, these young mothers could gain skills to move them toward economic self-sufficiency and that they could learn social problem-solving and active coping skills. We believed that life success is not beyond the reach of adolescent mothers. No doubt, these are assumptions that every educator and practitioner with heartfelt passion for their students to succeed, will share with us. Although research is always a journey, we are happy with our results so far. We are encouraged by the outcomes we have seen with adolescent mothers who have participated in the Taking Charge groups.

The current evidence, discussed in chapter 6, suggests that the Taking Charge curriculum helps adolescent mothers to develop life skills that they need to finish high school and move toward economic self-sufficiency. We continue to conduct outcome research and to build on this evidence. We invite other researchers and practitioner/researchers to help us in developing the promising evidence base of this group curriculum. We also invite each of you to test it out for yourself, using the methods that we suggest to collect data for your school. By all means, please ask the young women for refinements and improvements. We certainly asked them, and we welcome your comments for improvements, as well.

Finally, chapter 7 provides questions and answers that might be helpful to you as you apply the curriculum in the real world of your school. This chapter explores issues of adaptation. Taking Charge was always tested in the real world of public schools, and we have learned more and more about what is important in its implementation and the issues that schools face when using it. Like all learning, this is an ongoing process. Chapter 7 is a compilation of what we have learned from using this curriculum in schools and summarizes what school professionals and the pregnant and parenting participants of the program have taught us. It provides the nuts and bolts of practice wisdom. We expect that the users of this book will be able to contribute still more questions and answers.

Every School Can Use the Taking Charge Group Curriculum

We wrote this book to be a resource for every professional and paraprofessional who works with pregnant and parenting adolescents in public schools, as well as for those community-based health and mental health professionals who link with school systems. Every teacher and mental health professional will find this group curriculum useful in their work. Further, school support and mental health professionals are likely to find enthusiastic approval from other school personnel in offering this group curriculum.

The Taking Charge curriculum is among the least controversial programs for adolescent mothers, bringing together school and community stakeholders from all sides around the common concern of school achievement and economic self-sufficiency. The goals of the Taking Charge group are compatible with the abstinence-based focus being offered in many health and sex education programs. The curriculum places minimal strain on available resources. Being eminently compatible with basic instructional skills and knowledge, leading the group requires little additional training for teachers and school professionals. In fact, the detailed practice manual found in chapter 3 has made it feasible for social workers, counselors, school nurses, teachers, and even adolescent mothers and volunteers to lead the group effectively, thus extending program services in schools where student support services and mental health resources are limited. Studies of the curriculum have utilized staff, facilities, and materials considered standard in most school-based adolescent parent programs, suggesting that the group intervention can be incorporated relatively well into existing budgets. We are pleased to share the Taking Charge group curriculum with social workers, special education teachers, nurses, counselors, school psychologists, and other school practitioners who work with pregnant and parenting adolescents in schools.

Acknowledgments

First and foremost, we want to thank Oxford University Press for supporting this work. Our deepest gratitude goes to Joan H. Bossert and Maura Roessner for their support and direction during this project. We would also like to thank Dr. Albert Roberts for his encouragement and guidance. We give credit to the school social workers, teachers, counselors, nurses, graduate students, and especially to the adolescent mothers who participated in the testing of the Taking Charge curriculum. Finally, we would like to thank our family, friends, and colleagues who endured the process. Especially, we would like to mention Jim and Christina Franklin and Dr. Lois Marchino, who provided moral support and endless hours of editing.

Contents

Taking Charge

Chapter 1   *Critical Life Domains for Adolescent Mothers*

The way in which she negotiates her
life circumstances and rears her child
is determined by these ecologies.

P. L. Chase-Lansdale, J. Brooks-Gunn,
and R. L. Paikoff, "Research and programs
for adolescent mothers"

Welcome, reader! We are glad that you have decided to use the Taking
Charge group curriculum for adolescent mothers. This book serves as a
comprehensive leadership, training, and practice guide. It is important
for you to carefully read every chapter in order to prepare yourself to be a
leader or coleader for the Taking Charge group curriculum. Chapter 4 of
this book provides other important instructions on how to gain competencies in the clinical skills needed for effective leadership of the Taking
Charge groups. This first chapter opens the book by laying out the foundation for the life learning skills taught in the Taking Charge curriculum.
We use the term *life learning skills* because the skills supported in the
Taking Charge group are all reflected in behaviors and strategies practiced
in the day-to-day lives of adolescent mothers. Incentives and reinforce-
ments help to provide motivation while young mothers gain confidence
as they work toward mastery of new, sometimes difficult, skills.

Competent applications of life learning skills are based on the need to
address four critical life domains that adolescent mothers face in day-to-
day living: education, parenting, personal relationships, and employment/
career. Helping adolescent mothers to gain mastery and competence to
succeed in these four life domains is the essential learning element of
the Taking Charge group curriculum. These life domains, discussed in this
chapter, are based on empirical research that has repeatedly shown them
to be risk factors that impact the quality of life and life outcomes for adolescent mothers and their children. The curriculum presented in this book
helps young mothers learn social problem-solving and active coping skills

that they need to address and gain personal mastery within these four life domains.

Adolescent Motherhood and Life's Challenges

Moral beliefs and politics aside, the complexities of society and a burgeoning focus on sexuality has placed much of our adolescent population in a risky fast lane toward adult sexual experiences. One of the consequences for the past 3 decades is that, ready or not, adolescent women have been, and still are, getting pregnant and having babies.

A popular song from a few years ago, asks, "What's love got to do with it?" We ask a different question: What does *life* got to do with it? We think that life, as in lived experiences related to young age and early development, has a considerable bit to do with the challenges to self-sufficiency and success for adolescent mothers. Clearly, and reasonably so, many adolescent mothers lack experience with the daily tasks of child care, financial provision, time management, and negotiation of interpersonal relationships with fathers, families, healthcare professionals, and child care. They lack the years of life experience that older mothers draw upon to help them assume these complex functions. Even when young women have considerable experience with babies and child rearing, research studies suggest that it simply does not prepare them for the hardships and demands of mothering on their own (Clemmens, 2003).

For adolescent mothers still in the final stages of childhood and only beginning to develop adult skills, the responsibilities of parenting can be extremely difficult. The multiple demands of motherhood can become crisis-like for anyone who lacks life experiences and has limited resources, but can be especially so for adolescents. Caught in such an abrupt and premature transition, young mothers can easily lose grip on their immediate developmental life tasks such as school achievement and high school graduation, the management of personal relationships, and career preparation, not to mention the added dimension of parenting. Research suggests, however, that each of these life areas is critical to the mother's self-sufficiency and future success. For this reason, we selected these four to be the foundation and essential elements for the Taking Charge group curriculum.

These four life domains are the core components of the Taking Charge group. The life skills and experiential learning tasks of the curriculum are all structured around the foundation of these four domains. Chapter 3 explains this in detail.

So what is a life domain? One definition of the word *domain* is an area or activity in which one has leadership or influence. Another definition states that a domain is a territory where you exercise dominion or control. Building on these definitions, we define life domains as the territories of our lives in which we must have the knowledge, skills, and confidence to assume responsibility and "take charge" of those areas regardless of our life circumstances. Years of research tells us that how skillfully adolescent mothers are able to take charge of their lives and cope in the four life domains of education, personal relationships, parenting, and employment/career has the potential to make the biggest differences to their personal and economic success.

Such effective coping for adolescent mothers requires accelerated learning and mastery of new skills. In other words, adolescent mothers have entered the fast track of life experiences, and education professionals have to be prepared to help them do so successfully. The Taking Charge group curriculum is designed to help education professionals provide knowledge, cognitive tools, and confidence-enhancing experiences that will help adolescents develop mastery and competencies in the four life domains. The theoretical basis for this approach is discussed more in chapter 2. In this chapter, we lay a foundation for the essential elements of the four life domains.

Education

Of the four life domains discussed in this chapter, we believe that education is intertwined with the success of the other three and may be the most important life domain to influence. This is especially true if we hope to have an immediate impact on the direction of the mother's and the child's quality of life. In the next sections of this chapter, we explore why this is the case.

Chances are great that young mothers and their children are poor, and education is the first step out of poverty. Completing high school or a GED before the age of 20 is crucial to the future of every adolescent in America. For adolescent mothers, it not only helps to expand their immediate options, but contributes to their chances for future self-sufficiency and for keeping themselves and their children out of poverty (Martin, Hill, & Welch, 1998).

Literature that lists the deleterious effects that teen pregnancy has on both mother and child focuses, indeed, on the negative economic consequences. Although there is truth to some of the multiple risks of having a child when one is younger, this at-risk thinking can also perpetuate a myth that having a child in adolescence *causes* these young women to be poor. The truth is, however, that a large number of young mothers were living in impoverished families and communities before pregnancy occurred. A recent study of adolescent women living in poor families underscores this reality. Of 125 girls ages 15 to 19 living in families receiving Temporary Aid to Needy Families (TANF), more than 80 (65%) reported that they were sexually active, 35 (28%) had dropped out of school, and 22 (17%) were already mothers. They also reported mental health problems at about twice the rate of the national average for this age group (Boothroyd, Gomez, & Armstrong, 2005). Penalties of poverty such as these provoke questions about the core assumptions that society holds about the problems produced by adolescent pregnancy. The social and health problems and welfare dependency among adolescent mothers may exist to a large degree because they are poor and lack education, resources, and skills, not just because they gave birth to children at a young age. Poverty serves as a key factor in the social and behavioral difficulties of today's youths whether or not they become pregnant at a young age.

Taking on the responsibilities of motherhood at a young age, of course, does not make it any easier for a young woman to get out of poverty. Adolescent mothers find it more difficult to attain high school graduation than those who are not faced with the responsibilities of parenthood. Despite pregnancy prevention efforts in schools, some young women do not delay parenthood, whether accidentally or deliberately, even though it would be advantageous. We developed the Taking Charge curriculum to empower these young women to achieve in school despite their added challenges of early motherhood. We believe that taking charge of her own education is the first critical step to getting the young mother and her children up and out of poverty.

Research on the life experiences of adolescent mothers suggests that many of these mothers may share our convictions about the importance of education and the need to establish productive, self-sufficient lives for the sake of their children. Roosa (1986) found, for example, that a subgroup of mothers had every intention of finishing their education and had the family supports to do so. Other research suggests that adolescent pregnancy can be a transformative experience for young women and may even help them focus on a productive future. It is important for educational professionals to tap into the positive educational goals and aspirations of the young women and to help them develop direct experiences that will provide evidence that their personal feelings and dreams to finish their education is an achievable reality.

Clemmens (2003) reviewed several research studies suggesting that adolescent pregnancy can have a stabilizing affect on young women. The Taking Charge curriculum seeks to identify strengths in the educational domain, thus moving the young women toward the educational competence they desire. Diverse studies reviewed by Clemmens (2003) suggest the following:

1. Adolescents verbalize the importance of their education, especially since becoming mothers.

2. Participants express an awareness that education and training are needed to support their children as they now envisioned a future.

3. Adolescents are more goal-directed than they had been prior becoming mothers.

4. Mothers understand they need to stay in school and achieve their goals despite their past behaviors and histories.

5. Many of the adolescent participants in the studies develop a new sense of self with the baby providing the impetus to change, despite their impoverished pasts. The babies provided a tangible reason to stay in school and finish their studies to be better prepared for the future.

6. Many of the adolescent women in the studies possessed the motivation to complete high school and enroll in college.

Finally, this quote from the 1999 Deans Lake study illustrates the six points very well. This 17-year-old mother expresses her feelings about graduating from high school:

I only have one more year left. I'm going to be the first one that gradu-ates from high school and goes to college. . . . I want to go to Georgia, Georgia Tech. They've got a good school, plus I want to be around my color. I want to get away from my family. I want to make a differ-ence in my life and I want it to be good for my son (p. 69). (Cited in Clemmens, 2003, p. 5)

There is no doubt that many adolescent mothers are receptive to taking charge of their education even though it is not easy for them to focus on their schooling while trying to deal with diapers, bottles, and colicky babies. The Taking Charge group curriculum is designed to provide needed skills to help them actively problem solve and cope with the day-to-day challenges of life and at the same time keep their focus on their education. It is no secret that having a baby in adolescence is filled with stresses and distractions, and adolescent motherhood is a major factor influencing high school dropout for young women (Aloise-Young & Chavez, 2002). All the multiple tasks and roles required to be an adoles-cent, mother, and student result in many adolescent mothers electing to put their schooling on hold (Roosa, 1986). When it comes to choosing between school and their crying baby, school quickly loses out. Perhaps that is why school dropout is rampant among adolescent mothers, espe-cially those who become pregnant in their freshman or sophomore year.

Schools measure academic achievement by academic grades, test scores, and grade retention (Pearson & Banerji, 1993), which are affected by factors that haunt adolescent mothers, such as absenteeism, social iso-lation, and discipline problems (Mayer, Mitchell, Clementi, & Clement-Robertson, 1993). School professionals are familiar with the fact that absenteeism generally increases once pregnancy occurs and is not likely to improve after the baby is born. Increased absenteeism and social iso-lation are major barriers to academic achievement and contributors to school dropout for adolescent mothers.

Research suggests that reasons for school dropout among young mothers tend to fall into three categories: school, personal, and family/sociocultural (see box 1.1).

1. Some school-related issues that appear to affect dropout include rigid school requirements for attendance, minimal encouragement from school staff to continue in school, and lack of consideration for individual needs (C. Black & DeBlassie, 1985; Kissman, 1998).

2. Personal reasons are often related to making other adult transitions at the same time that the adolescent becomes a mother, such as moving away from her family, getting a job, or getting married (Hayes, 1987). Indications are that if the young mother marries during or soon after pregnancy, the probability of her dropping out increases (Mott, 1986; Rumberger, 1987). Finally, the age of adolescents at the time they become pregnant appears to be an important factor in school dropout. Research strongly indicates that mothers 15 and younger are less likely to complete high school than those over age 15 (DeBolt, Pasley, & Kreutzer, 1990). Data from 6,300 women between ages 14 and 22, for example, reported that 55% of the women who became pregnant at 15 or older dropped out of school, whereas 70% of those younger than 15 had dropped out (Mott & Marsiglio, 1985).

Box 1.1 **Circumstances of School Dropout Among Adolescent Mothers**

School-Related	Personal	Family/Sociocultural
■ Rigid school attendance requirements	■ Moves away from family	■ Receives strong family and social network support to drop out
■ Minimal encouragement from school staff to remain in school	■ Gets a job	
	■ Gets married	■ No support network to help with child care and other parenting-related responsibilities
■ Lack of accommodation to individual needs	■ Is 15 or younger at time of pregnancy	
■ Being below grade level	■ Has a repeat pregnancy	
■ High absenteeism		

The Taking Charge group curriculum helps school professionals purposefully intervene into issues like absenteeism, and social isolation. Taking Charge is designed to offer the extra social support and rewards that might be needed for persisting toward educational achievement even when times are tough. Additionally, the solution-focused and task-centered approach to the curriculum allows for a detailed exploration of the personal and family issues that are most important in the young women's social lives and that may also prevent her from coming to school. The interventions within the Taking Charge curriculum that are specifically designed to increase attendance and school progress are examined in more detail in chapters 2, 3, and 4.

3. Finally, it is important for educators and school-support professionals to always be reminded that adolescents often drop out of school for a host of reasons that have nothing to do with academics or their ability to perform in school or even the issues of the baby or the pregnancy itself. Complex social, health, mental health, and family issues are often linked with why adolescents become pregnant and leave school prematurely. The proverbial question of which came first, the chicken or the egg, applies to many of these problem issues, and it is hard to sort out what issue came first. We summarize a few challenges that contribute to school dropout next, and discuss how each of these may be intertwined with being pregnant and parenting.

Dropout, Mental Health Problems, and Pregnancy

Mental health problems that lead to school difficulties and dropout tend to occur more frequently in students who are also facing other social or health challenges (Boothroyd, Gomez, & Armstrong, 2005), including those who are pregnant or parenting. Every year, one in five youths in the general population experiences symptoms of a *DSM-IV-TR* disorder (U.S. Department of Health and Human Services, 1999). Depression and posttraumatic stress disorder, however, are substantially higher among pregnant adolescents than the general adolescent population (Corcoran, Franklin, & Bennett, 2000; Franklin, Corcoran, & Harris, 2004).

Adolescents who are pregnant and parenting have high rates of sexual abuse (Luster & Small, 1997; Stock, Bell, Boyer, & Connell, 1997). The resulting trauma from sexual abuse, which often develops into full-blown posttraumatic stress disorder, greatly complicates the lives of young mothers and their children. Research tells us that sexual abuse may also be linked to many of the behavioral risks associated with adolescent pregnancy. Large-scale surveys indicate, for example, that teens who have been sexually abused tend to have had sex by age 15, have had more partners, failed to use birth control at last intercourse, and were more likely to have been pregnant or caused a pregnancy (Luster & Small, 1997; Raj, Silverman, & Amaro, 2000; Stock et al., 1997).

In addition to their specific mental health challenges, adolescent mothers are not exempt from the critical problems and stressors that pervade the general teenage social environment. Homicide is the second leading cause of death for adolescents, and suicide is third (Roberts & Yeager, 2005). More adolescents are infected now with HIV/AIDS than in 2000 (Hopson, 2006). Thirty-seven percent of high school students report being involved in school violence (Kann et al., 1998), and 14% even report carrying weapons to school (Josephson Institute on Ethics, 2001, cited in Mattaini, 2006). U.S. cities report an estimated 31,000 adolescent gangs (Moore & Terrett, 1998), with gang presence in schools increasing from 15% in 1989 to 28% in 1995 (Thornberry & Burch, 1997). Adolescents who are pregnant and parenting are certainly affected by these teenage problems and, in fact, appear to become even more vulnerable to situational stress.

When adolescent mothers are experiencing mental health challenges, they need assistance from school or community mental health professionals. The Taking Charge group curriculum is designed to help mothers to develop skills in problem-focused coping and to guide them in working through whatever life challenges they may be struggling with in their day-to-day lives. The participants are able to set their own goals, and the curriculum is open to outside supports and interventions. The philosophy of the curriculum is solution solving, and that leads the young woman to come up with her own solution and to work through proven steps of social problem solving to accomplish her goals. "Whatever it takes" would be an accepted motto.

For this reason, Taking Charge will begin where the mother is, at her level or stage of change and motivation, as long as she commits to follow the intervention and participate in the group. We have seen many young women who struggle with mental health challenges find the needed mental health help from outside sources while in the Taking Charge groups. We believe that the experience of being a mother may even make the young woman more motivated toward this help. Williams and Vine (1999) found in their research that some adolescent mothers used their motherhood experience as a transitional life experience to break free from abusive and impoverished life backgrounds, for example.

Dropout, Drug Abuse, and Pregnancy

Although drug abuse appears to have decreased generally among American youths over the past decade, it remains a present and serious problem for scores of at-risk adolescent groups (DiGiovanni, 2006). The relationship among drug abuse, pregnancy, and school dropout appears to be so complex that drug abuse may be both an outcome and a predictor of pregnancy and dropout. A study by Hallfors et al. (2002) found that truancy, low GPA, and recent sexual activity were strong predictors of drug use, with truancy and sexual activity being stronger than low GPA. Conversely, sources cited by Aloise-Young and Chavez (2002, p. 539) indicate that high school dropouts are more likely to use drugs (Beauvais, Chavez, & Oetting, 1996). Evidence strongly links substance use and sexuality (Perkins, Luster, Villarreal, & Small, 1998). According to Franklin and Corcoran (1999), substance use increases high-risk adolescent sexual behavior in at least four ways:

1. It increases susceptibility to acting on sexual impulses without considering possible consequences.
2. It encourages poor choice of partners.
3. It adds to lack of contraceptive use.
4. It often renders the teen unable to remember sexual experiences.

When adolescent mothers face issues of substance use, outside agencies and interventions beyond the school are often needed. The Taking Charge group curriculum offers useful skills for the mother to begin to explore her drug use behavior in relation to successes, failures, and major life goals. Fortunately, the social problem-solving and coping skills taught in the Taking Charge curriculum have been found to be effective interventions with drug-abusing and other antisocial youths when applied to those behaviors (e.g., Botvin & Botvin, 1992; Hogue & Liddle, 1999; McWhirter & Page, 1999), and our clinical experience tells us that they offer an added benefit to adolescent mothers in the Taking Charge curriculum who are substance abusing, as well.

Personal Relationships

Personal relationships are the second life domain that research suggests serves as a risk factor for adolescent mothers and impacts their future. The Taking Charge group curriculum actively addresses this domain as being an important area in which the mother needs to develop knowledge, skills, and confidence to assume responsibility and "take charge" of that area regardless of her life circumstances. Recall from our previous discussion that this is our definition of a life domain.

In the following paragraphs, we want to enlighten you as to why personal relationships are so important and vital to the adolescent mother's well-being and the well-being of her child. We will explore personal relationships in their various roles: parental and family relationships, peers, and the relationship with the baby's father. First, we want to point out that personal relationships are vital to mothers of any age, and particularly to those in adolescence. Friendships with others near their age are considered essential to teenagers, and so is the continued protection and support of parents and family. Experimenting on varying levels with sexual intimacy, often by having a boyfriend or girlfriend, takes on primary importance in adolescence.

As important as all these different relationships are to the growth and well-being of an adolescent woman, experts agree that they are all likely to change if she becomes pregnant and has a baby. Some relationships may remain supportive and be resilient enough to weather the changes, but just as often personal relationships can go in directions that create problems and stress for the adolescent mother and her child (Bogat et al., 1998; Martin, Hill, & Welch, 1998; Uno, Florsheim, & Uchino, 1998). So, personal relationships are vital and important, and may even be necessary for social support, emotional health, and economic survival. Conversely, they are also often a major cause of stress and conflict for the adolescent mother and her family. We will explore these issues in more detail from the advantage point of research, and it will become clear why this life domain is so important to the adolescent mother and should be addressed in a curriculum that is serious about preparing adolescent mothers for a successful future.

Parental and Family Relationships

Studies on adolescent mothers and their families give results that on the surface appear to be conflicting but may simply mirror the complexity of relationships and circumstances between adolescents and their parents. For example, numerous studies have found that adolescent mothers consistently identify their mothers and other family members as a source of social support (Richardson, Barbour, & Bubenzer, 1995; Wasserman, Brunelli, & Rauh, 1990). For example, Paskiewicz (2001) found that adolescent mothers described their mothers as being helpful mentors in supporting their transition to motherhood. Also, even if their relationships were at times conflicted, the tangible and emotional support offered by the grandmothers, for example, helped the adolescent mothers perform well in school, and grow as individuals.

Yet other studies suggest that although family relationships can provide positive support, they can also cause strain and lowered adjustment to pregnancy and parenting (Bogat et al., 1998; Kalil, Spencer, Spieker, & Gilchrist, 1998; Martin et al., 1998). One study found that adolescent mothers identified family relationships as their greatest source of stress (Stern & Zevon, 1990). Another found that adolescent mothers with the greatest depressive symptoms were those who lived with their mothers and often other family members in an environment of high family conflict and stress (Kalil et al., 1998). Still others conclude that although family and maternal support may be beneficial to the adolescent mother, it is often difficult for her to accept (Nitz, Ketterlinus, & Brandt, 1995, as cited in Bunting & McAuley, 2004).

The relationship between adolescents and their parents, particularly daughters with their mothers, is complex, and school professionals have to be prepared to help the young woman to build on strengths in those relationships, as well as understand and resolve problem areas that might interfere with a productive future for the mother and her child. Clearly, the quality and availability of the support from the adolescent's mother or grandmother is important to her own parenting and her immediate economic stability (Unger & Wandersman, 1988; Wasserman, Brunelli, & Rauh, 1990) as well as her mental well-being and general adjustment during and after pregnancy (Kalil et al., 1998). This makes mother-daughter relationships an important area to assess and strengthen and an essential area that may either enhance or sabotage school adjustment, as well. For example, how many adolescent mothers' schooling has been preserved by the child-care roles and support of their mothers or grand-mothers?

Even though there is considerable research on adolescent mothers and their families, most studies do not adequately address the developmental dynamics of the mother-daughter relationship (Bunting & McAuley, 2004). It is largely through studying ordinary mother-daughter relationships during adolescence that we learn something about the impact of these relationships for adolescent mothers. Adolescence is described as the most difficult of times between mothers and daughters in the American culture, even though not all mothers and daughters appear to experience great conflict (Kenemore & Spira, 1996). For the adolescent's mother, this period requires continued care and nurturing as well as managing the increasing ambiguity of her relationship with her adolescent daughter (Elson, 1986). As the daughter moves toward adulthood, her changes must be accommodated by her mother, and there is a gradual transformation in the mother-daughter relationship (Chodorow, 1989). If circumstances or interpersonal resources cannot accommodate this reshaping of their relationship, the two can become stuck in perpetual conflict or cold distance.

The strain that an adolescent pregnancy brings to the mother and the daughter can either forge their relationship deeper or break it. Like clay in a fire, the relationship emerges as a stronger, healthier adult unity or a broken vessel in need of repair. The time in the fire, during the pregnancy and in the early years after the birth of the baby, can be a difficult experience for each. In our experience with young mothers participating in Taking Charge groups, more than 50% identified the relationships with their own mothers as their most challenging relationship (Table 6.7). Chapter 6 provides some interesting case studies that illustrate some of these struggles. The Taking Charge group curriculum provides a process for young women to resolve issues with their mothers and their families of origin and, when necessary, to sever destructive relationships in ways that are healthy for the mother and the baby.

Peer Relationships

Adolescents with strong peer friendships have greater self-esteem, less depression, and better adjustment to school (Berndt & Savin-Williams, 1996). Research is conflicted about the nature of peer relationships among adolescent mothers. Although earlier research determined that peer relationships weakened or ended after pregnancy and the birth of a child (Barth & Schinke, 1984; Panzarine, 1986), a more recent study (Richardson et al., 1995) found that peers provided moderate levels of support and were seen by the young mothers as being more emotionally supportive than family members. Although they reach different conclusions, all these results uphold the need for adolescent mothers to have viable peer relationships. Thus, it is clearly important to include friendships in social skills building interventions with young mothers. The Taking Charge curriculum uses a process-oriented, task-centered group structure (discussed more in chapters 2 and 3) that allows adolescent mothers to build a social network within the group, as well as enhance peer relationships in other parts of their lives. The personal relationship domain encourages the adolescents to develop social skills and friendships within the group and in school, as well as supports them in mastering personal relationship skills.

Relationship With Father of Baby

Much of what we know from research about adolescent fathers deals with factors that lead to adolescents becoming fathers (Resnick, Chambliss, & Blum, 1993) rather than the relationship they have with their child and its mother (Christmon, 1990; Miller, 1994). Although some research on social support for adolescent mothers omits the baby's father altogether (e.g., Richardson et al., 1995), mothers in other studies identify the baby's father as an important source of support (de Anda & Becerra, 1984; Wasserman, Brunelli, & Rauh, 1990). When the adolescent mother's family of origin is conflicted or stressed and has a negative impact on her and her child, researchers identify the baby's father as a viable alternative resource (Kalil et al., 1998; Wasserman et al., 1990). Some of the issues regarding the fathers of the babies of adolescent mothers are complicated by the fact that many of these fathers are adults rather than adolescents (Leitenberg & Saltzman, 2000).

Research findings offer mixed results regarding the level of support the fathers of babies of adolescent mothers provide for their children. Ninety-three percent of the adolescent mothers in one sample believed that the fathers should provide financial support and participate in raising the child, whereas only 58% of the fathers in that study agreed (Rhein et al., 1997). Other studies validate that at least a third of adolescent fathers provide good financial support and maintain contact with the mother and child (Kalil, Ziol-Guest, & Coley, 2005). In our studies of the Taking Charge curriculum, 35% of participants' relationship goals related to the baby's father, and 36% of the parenting goals related to some aspect of coparenting with the baby's father (Table 6.7). Because one of the most critical links to successful adjustment of adolescent mothers is a strong support system, when a large portion of young mothers perceive the father of their baby as an important source of support, it is important to focus on relationship skills with young mothers that can preserve and enhance that relationship. The relationship domain of the Taking Charge group curriculum provides such a focus.

Parenting

Parenting is the third critical life domain that serves as a risk factor for the adolescent mother and her baby. Much literature has been devoted to this risk factor because when people think about adolescent mothers, they often worry that young mothers lack parenting skills and that this lack of skills may potentially damage their children. A stereotype in the minds of some people in society is the image of a teenage mom as a person who commits acts of child abuse and neglect. Parenting and taking care of their children is almost always on the minds of the adolescent mothers, as well. They worry about taking care of the basic needs of their children, like having enough diapers, finding child care, and addressing concerns like "Is she warm enough?" and "What do I do when he gets a fever?" and things that most mothers worry about. Like any other mother, a teenage mother can be a better parent when she has emotional, financial, and social supports in place.

Our definition of a life domain really stands a challenge here because, as we have said, life domains are the territories of our lives in which we must have the knowledge, skills, and confidence to assume responsibilities and "take charge" of those areas regardless of our life circumstances. Consequently, being very young and lacking life experiences must not ultimately prevent us from being a good parent. This assumption raises many questions, however, that we will address next. Is it possible to transcend the negative health consequences of a woman having a baby at a very young age? Are adolescent mothers destined to be irresponsible, abusive, and neglectful parents? And how can the Taking Charge group curriculum possibly help teenage mothers with the monumental task of parenthood? First, we turn to the question of health risks.

Health Risks and Development

Obstetric health risks to adolescent mothers include such conditions as toxemia, anemia, cephalopelvic disproportion, and hypertension. Adverse health risks to the child include low birth weight, prematurity, and infant mortality. These conditions may be overly attributed in the early literature to the physiologic immaturity of the adolescent. It is now recognized that social and economic factors such as poverty, single-parent status, and poor prenatal care also play a large role in poorer health outcomes, and when adolescents receive good medical care, their risk for negative health outcomes substantially decreases (Stevens-Simon & Nelligan, 1998; Turner, Grindstaff, & Phillips, 1990).

The most important factor related to health and birth complications is the lack of adequate prenatal care, especially in adolescents under age 15 from low-income families (Opuni, Smith, Arvey, & Solomon, 1994). Ongoing relationships with health professionals, such as visiting nurses, have also been shown to reduce repeat pregnancies in adolescents and to have favorable impacts in other areas of the adolescent mother's life (Seitz & Apfel, 1999). It is extremely important for pregnant and parenting adolescents to receive excellent prenatal and postnatal care. Some studies suggest that adolescent prenatal behaviors, such as poor eating habits, increase health risks for mother and child (Levy, Perhats, Nash-Johnson, & Welter, 1992; Marques & McKnight, 1991). A high incidence of drug use, especially in the early months most vital to fetal brain and organ development, is also a concern (Marques & McKnight, 1991).

Public school and public health resources can make a big difference in the health outcomes of mother and child. Prenatal health programs and services are most often developed and staffed by nurses or public health professionals and, until recently, operated in clinics or hospitals (Covington, Carl, Daley, Cushing, & Churchill, 1998; Stevens-Simon, O'Connor, & Bassford, 1994). A growing number of health services and clinics in high schools and special education settings in the past decades (Lear, 2006), however, show an increase in school-based programs that promote health for both mothers and their babies. These programs result in favorable outcomes for both mother and baby.

Currently there are more than 1,500 school-based health clinics across the country (Center for Health and Healthcare in Schools, 2007). Interventions that focus primarily on health outcomes for mother and child often impact or directly link to psychosocial and educational goals, as well, again showing the connection among physical-social-psychological-educational factors with adolescent mothers. Let us consider a case in point. Goals of the Northeast Adolescent project (NEAP) in Houston, for example, were to increase prenatal and postpartum compliance and to lower the incidence of premature births and low birth weight. The program evaluation for NEAP showed that it also had a significant impact on school retention (Opuni et al., 1994). In another study, the goal of home visits and nurse-instructed classes on contraception and infant development was to reduce repeat childbearing, a factor also linked to negative education and economic outcomes (Seitz & Apfel, 1999). These types of programs have been found to be especially effective when nurse home-visitation programs are included. Our clinical experience in schools tells us that these types of health interventions link well and complement the Taking Charge group curriculum. Below, we describe how the connection works.

The health-care issues of child and mother are important to the future success of both, and the Taking Charge group curriculum addresses the health-care issues from the social problem-solving perspective. The group works on health-care issues by empowering the mother to increase and improve her communication and cooperation with health-care professionals and resources, and to become more confident in these exchanges. Research supports this experiential/mastery approach as one of the most effective ways to impact the health-care issues of mother and child. We found in our clinical and case study experiences with Taking Charge groups that health-care issues were greatly impacted by personal relationship issues and, in turn, that the health of the baby coupled with personal relationship issues were common reasons for why mothers missed school. Chapter 6 summarizes the finding of these case studies. The Taking Charge curriculum encourages active, social problem solving toward healthy living through supporting the mother toward self-sufficiency, including being able to manage the health-care needs of herself and her baby.

One way health care can be addressed in Taking Charge from a social perspective is in the personal relationship domain, for example. As stated, some mothers may be blocked from good health care by personal habits or unhealthy relationships that interfere with their schooling and appropriate decisions toward a healthy lifestyle. Others may have relationship difficulties with health-care professionals who are interfering with their health care, and these relationship issues may need to be resolved before the mother and the baby get the medical attention they need.

Parenting is another area in which health care can be addressed. Well-baby checkups, as well as all of the medical needs of a child, are important parental responsibilities. However, because a child's medical appointments require frequent open time slots, this can impact the mother's school attendance, for example. These types of health-care issues may require special planning and problem solving and help from the school to resolve. For a mother with a disabled child, her ongoing relationship with the health-care system may become very important in her life. When this happens, she may need ongoing help in managing all the ensuing complications with her school schedule. Further, the employment/career life domain, to be discussed below, may also impact health care. Mothers may lack the financial resources to seek needed health care and need to problem solve though that area.

Adolescent Mothers and Child Abuse

Unfortunately, parenting programs for adolescents continue to focus heavily on child abuse and neglect (Stevens-Simon & Nelligan, 1998), even though credible research now concludes that abuse and neglect may be due more to conditions such as poverty and single parenthood than to young age per se (Deal & Holt, 1998). Several good studies on the parenting practices of mothers with infants have concluded that teenage mothers are as nurturing and warm toward their infants as older mothers, and they have similar proportions of securely attached infants (Benn & Saltz, 1989; Ward, Carlson, Plunkett, & Kessler, 1988). Their primary shortcoming in overall parenting during infancy may be that they talk less to their babies and provide less stimulation than older mothers (Culp, Appelbaum, Osofsky, & Levy, 1989), a dynamic that may be key in less developed cognitive functioning later on. Of the two, child neglect may be of more concern with adolescent mothers than child abuse. Studies show less difference between abusive and nonabusive mothers than between neglectful mothers and nonneglectful mothers (see box 1.2; Zuravin & DiBlasio, 1996).

Box 1.2 **Characteristics of Abusive Versus Neglectful Adolescent Mothers**

Abusive Mothers

■ Own mother had emotional problems

■ Were not attached to own mother

■ Were loners as children

■ Family received public assistance

Neglectful Mothers

■ Were sexually abused

■ Had multiple caretakers

■ Ran away from home

■ Had trouble with the law

■ Had prior miscarriage or abortion

■ Completed fewer grades in school

■ Had a premature, low birth weight baby

Source: Zuravin & DiBlasio (1996).

Abusers are more likely than nonabusers to have a mother with emotional problems, less attachment to their mother figure, to have been "loners" as children, and to have lived in a family that received public assistance. On the other hand, neglecters, more than nonneglecters, are likely to have traumatic childhood histories that include sexual abuse, trouble with the law, and multiple caretakers. Neglecters are also more likely to have had a miscarriage or abortion prior to their first birth, to have their first child at a younger age, to have had a premature or low birth weight first child, and to have completed fewer grades in school than either nonabusive or abusive mothers. Zuravin and DiBlasio (1996) concluded in their study that the maternal characteristics linked to abuse and neglect in adolescent mothers are nearly the same as those found 20 years earlier in older mothers by Parke and Collmer (1975).

What this information tells us is that the adolescent pregnancy alone is not what puts a young woman at risk for child abuse or neglect and that school professionals should look for risk factors and be alert to abuse and neglect in this group of students in the same way they would be in any population. At the same time, expect that the adolescent mothers will love and nurture their children and are similar to all first-time mothers. Like most first-time mothers, they need a little hand-holding to calm fears, education about child development, a lot of social and emotional support, and some time off from parenting for good behavior. Most mothers usually know what areas they need help with in rearing their children. Instead of presuming the mothers' parenting needs, the Taking Charge group curriculum starts with the assumption that these adolescent mothers are first-time mothers who want to be good parents and allows the mothers to set goals and explore the parenting skills they need to strengthen to become better parents. Group leaders proceed to reinforce those skills in the context of the mother's daily life.

Keeping a Balanced Perspective on Adolescent Mothering

Research suggests that having a baby as an adolescent may negatively affect a child's development, but we should remember that issues of poverty and social class are inextricably linked. We cannot conclude from the research evidence that adolescent mothers are ineffective parents.

It is most important to recognize that the consequences of the mother's age also operate through her education, knowledge of childrearing, social support, and family structure, size, and income. When mothers who are poor are provided health services, for example, the negative health affects often decrease or even disappear. When socioeconomic factors are considered, young mothers do not appear any more likely to abuse or neglect their children than older mothers. Although we do not minimize the need for interventions focused on parenting with young mothers, we strongly believe in focusing on the specific skills and strengths the mothers already possess, as well as those that the mothers identify that may need to be strengthened in order to become better parents. We believe it is essential for us to put more of our attention on the educational and socioeconomic risk factors that we know from research to be important to the mother and child's successful life outcomes.

Employment/Career

Employment/career is the fourth life domain that is a risk factor for the adolescent mother and her child. This life domain is most important to the overall quality of life for child and mother because employment provides the money and resources that mothers and their children need to live in our society and be productive citizens. Recall one final time that a life domain is a territory for which we must take responsibility and take charge regardless of our personal circumstances. This life domain of employment, however, is extremely sensitive to personal circumstances such as age and education. It is not possible, for example, for us to take complete charge of our employment in a short-term solution. Employment or career is something that happens across our life and has strong developmental considerations. What may be considered a good job at one point in our life, may not be considered a good job at another point. What matters most is quality of life and being able to be self-sufficient for where we are at different ages and stages of our life cycle.

The Taking Charge group curriculum aims to support knowledge, planning skills, and experiential tasks that will move the mother toward career planning and self-sufficiency. It takes patience, persistence, and time to stay on that track, and young women need to be assured that persisting through the difficulties is a normal life experience. Taking Charge will be a beginning, not an ending, in the process of mastering life across this critical domain. Employment and career will be ongoing and changing experiences throughout life. It is normal to expect some setbacks, failures, and adversities along the path of our growth. What is important, when that happens, is that we cope with it and keep progressing toward our goals.

We liken this to the analogy of playing a board game, the game of Life. In this board game, shortcuts like skipping college and going directly to work may not lead to the best ends, and setbacks like having a child early may not lead to the worst ends either. When we have a promising education and a career, we may reach the end of the game, many years later, as the winner, even if we draw many bad cards along the way. It can happen! It only takes time to get older and to complete our education and to land a better job, and move down the road of life. One day the children will be grown and our adolescent mothers will still be very young and have many years of life to pursue their job and careers, for example. Think about that outcome!

The Taking Charge group curriculum teaches a set of active, social problem-solving and coping skills that prepare adolescent mothers for the struggles of real life and the adversities that we have to overcome to become self-sufficient in employment. Our overall success at employment, however, is also related to things outside our immediate social control like socioeconomic background, race, and gender. We certainly believe that educational professionals must be proactive in trying to change the conditions of society that make it harder for adolescent women of color to be treated with equal respect and employed fairly, for example. At the same time, the approach of the Taking Charge group curriculum is for all young women to possess the knowledge, skills, and self-confidence to face and actively cope with such conditions until they are changed. In other words, it strives to change what can be changed but also to meet life as it is, in the present, and to find ways to problem-solve and excel despite oppressive social conditions that might make it difficult for these mothers to do so. We are very aware, however, that economic stability is the most challenging aspect of adolescent pregnancy because, as has already been discussed at length, many pregnant adolescents are poor and come from impoverished families and communities. To take charge of this life territory requires a good job with an income that raises one well above the poverty line.

Of course, it is an extraordinary and unrealistic challenge for teen moms who have a baby in arms—or for any teenager, for that matter—to find employment at that level. So, we have to focus on that reality and think of education first, along with moving into the first job for the older adolescents (16 and older), with more progressive planning steps toward promising employment. Younger adolescents (15 and younger) are in for a longer journey in high school coupled with job experimentation. The Taking Charge curriculum was developed primarily for schools to reinforce positive educational outcomes for adolescent mothers. Yet, many adolescent mothers by necessity are thrust early into the world of work and may work and go to school at the same time. They piece together sources of income from fast-food jobs, the baby's father, their mother or grandmother (who may also poor), and whatever public assistance they can get. And, yes, maybe even a few have some income for which they would not want to tell a school professional about the source. It is a day-to-day struggle to make ends meet and to have enough, diapers, formula, food, and transportation to survive. Yet, most mothers are determined to make it work for the sake of their baby and their own welfare.

The Taking Charge group curriculum addresses employment at different stages of development (e.g., current employment and future desired employment and plans). The overarching goal of Taking Charge curriculum is to help adolescent mothers prepare for the self-sufficiency of themselves and their children. We suspect that some educational professionals might be concerned about our singular focus on this goal. Most educators will recognize the goal as being obviously very American and Western, and may be concerned that the self-sufficiency emphasis will be in conflict with culturally diverse American families and many immigrant groups that have non-Western worldviews. We certainly recognize that this is the case and address how to work with unavoidable value conflicts around self-sufficiency and diverse cultural beliefs in chapter 5. We believe the self-sufficiency goal is pragmatic, and Taking Charge was originally designed to help young Mexican American and immigrant women reach that goal.

We affirm the inherent human rights for adolescent mothers and their children to live a life free from poverty and oppression and to reach those goals in an American society. We further believe that they will have to create a life of economic self-sufficiency in order to be free. We certainly want to see them get as much help as possible toward that end, and we are convinced that one of the best places for this assistance is the public schools. Schools that provide the Taking Charge group curriculum and other support programs for parenting and pregnant adolescents create opportunities for young women to transcend the difficulties of adolescent pregnancy and find a self-sufficient life and career path.

What We Know About Employment and Economic Stability of Adolescent Mothers

We know less about the vocational choices and employment histories of adolescent mothers than about other circumstances of their lives. We do know that women with a high school diploma will make, on average, $7,000 more per year by current economic standards than women without a high school diploma (National At-Risk Education Network, 2006). Thus, a teen mother who graduates from high school is likely to earn at least $300,000 more over her lifetime than a teen mother who drops out of high school. This fact alone gives us renewed motivation to help young mothers stay in school and graduate. Focusing specifically on *how* they will support themselves and their children beyond high school may be equally as important in this time of diminishing resources for young parents.

In addition to education, these are other important conditions known to influence income and employment:

- *Age at first and second pregnancies* (Seitz & Apfel, 1993). Younger adolescents have poorer outcomes.

- *Education of parents* (Forste & Tienda, 1992). The more education of parents the better outcome.

- *Presence or absence of one or both parents* (Balcazar, Peterson, & Krull, 1997). The relationship of the mother has already been discussed as an important protective factor.

- *Parental supervision* (Balcazar, Peterson, & Krull, 1997).

We want to take this opportunity to point out specifically that implicit throughout the Taking Charge group curriculum is the use of research information and knowledge about risk factors. This information is included in order to empower the young women with knowledge as they plan contingencies to overcome obstacles or put in place protective factors that could make up the differences. Knowledge is used as a tool to empower—not to disempower or to communicate that you are not going to be able to have a good outcome because a condition exists; such would be the case with the risk factors above. So, for example, being young does not have to lead to a negative outcome if one knows that this puts you more at risk. You simply have to be more prepared and will have to work harder than older women in the same circumstances. It is obviously going to take longer and a lot more effort and assistance to get you through school, but you can still make it.

As box 1.3 shows, the sources of economic support received by young mothers earlier in life can predict the level of self-earned income later in adulthood (Corcoran, Gordon, Laren, & Solon, 1992; Duncan & Yeung, 1995). Box 1.3 identifies income sources that do and do not have bearing on self-earned income later in life. As the box identifies, early work experiences are important and should not be minimized. All work should be respected as having value for future economic stability, and the Taking Charge curriculum values the work experiences of adolescents in this way. Drawing on developmental theory, the Taking Charge group curriculum addresses all beginning work experiences with employment as an opportunity for the adolescent to explore and learn vital skills needed to be a success in the world of work.

Box 1.3	Sources of Early Economic Support and Later Self-Earned Income

No Impact on Later Self-Earned Income	*Increases Later Self-Earned Income*
■ Public assistance	■ Sharing housing with another family, including family of origin
■ Food stamps, Medicaid, housing assistance	■ Early work experience
■ Financial support from relatives	■ Child support from baby's father

Source: Sandfort & Hill (1996).

First jobs are important jobs for adolescents. They are learning and bringing these growth experiences into the Taking Charge group so that they can set goals to improve their job performance and skills in the present, and start to identify what kind of job and career that they ultimately want to pursue. Taking Charge focuses on building self-confidence and self-efficacy for the young woman to believe in her ability to be a good worker. Taking Charge also provides some additional learning experiences and information about the world of work and the career paths for the older women in the group while supporting the plans of the younger ones. This is individually tailored to each group and situation. Chapters 3 and 4 investigate this approach in more detail.

Summary

In this chapter, we discussed the four critical life domains of education, personal relationships, parenting, and employment/career faced by adolescent mothers. These life domains are essential elements of the Taking Charge group curriculum and are based on empirical research on risk factors that impact the self-sufficiency of adolescent mothers and their overall quality of life. A life domain is a life territory in which we must have the knowledge, skills, and confidence to assume responsibility and "take charge" of that area regardless of our life circumstances. These four critical life domains are risk factors that adolescent mothers struggle with on a daily basis and need accelerated, advanced skills to address.

Years of research tells us that the skill with which adolescent mothers are able to take charge of their lives and cope in the four life territories of education, personal relationships, parenting, and employment/career has the potential to make the biggest differences to their personal and economic success. Such effective coping requires an accelerated approach to learning and mastery of new skills. In other words, these young women have entered the fast track of life experiences, and educators must be prepared to help them keep up successfully. The Taking Charge group curriculum was designed to help educational professionals provide knowledge, skills, and confidence-building exercises that will help adolescents develop mastery and competencies in the four life domains.

Chapter 2   *Theories and Evidence Supporting Development of the Taking Charge Group Curriculum*

The Taking Charge group curriculum is a multimodal, brief, cognitive-behavioral curriculum. This intervention was developed within a developmental and strengths-based, solution-focused framework, utilizing the strengths, resources, life goals, and developmental tasks of adolescent mothers. The curriculum is presented as an 8- to 12-week, school-based intervention offered within a task-centered group. The tasks of the group focus on learning new cognitions and behaviors that strengthen the adolescent mother's active problem-solving and coping skills. In turn, these new skills are used to gain better mastery and self-sufficiency across the four critical life domains, education, personal relationships, parenting, and employment/career, which were discussed in chapter 1. Our goal was to build a curriculum that was strengths-oriented and mastery-based, and that could help adolescent mothers learn to accelerate the skills needed to achieve excellence in the aforementioned four life domains. See box 2.1 for a summary of the theoretical basis of the Taking Charge curriculum's intervention components.

This chapter explains the theoretical and empirical basis of the Taking Charge group curriculum, including its developmental and strengths-based, solution-focused frameworks, and the life skills interventions of active, social problem solving and coping. These life skills are taught to accelerate learning across the four life domains and are based on social learning and cognitive-behavioral interventions. The importance and potential effectiveness of these types of skills with adolescent mothers is discussed. This chapter further explains the importance of the task-centered group approach that is used to teach the cognitive-behavioral skills to the adolescent mothers. Finally, we discuss why we believe that brief group programs like the Taking Charge group curriculum are important to schools and can be effective in a school setting.

Box 2.1   **Major Theoretical Components for the Taking Charge Curriculum**

---

1. *Goal setting across the four critical life domains*—education, personal relationships, parenting, and career/employment—is based on research that says these areas are risk factors and are most influential in the long-term life outcomes with adolescent mothers. Goal setting across the life domains increases acquisition and mastery of life skills, thus reducing risk factors and improving positive life outcomes.

2. *Developmental theory framework*, including concepts from role theory, guide understanding and take into account the developmental factors of adolescence that heavily influence the needs, skills, and social context of adolescent mothers, and thus heavily impact the long-term well-being of them and their children.

3. *Strengths-based, solution-focused brief therapy framework* establishes a focus on strengths, resources, and goals that facilitate developmental learning, mastery, and self-confidence in the adolescents as they learn how to develop their own solutions. This approach has shown promise in work with dropout prevention (Franklin, Kim & Tripodi, 2006).

4. *Theory of stress and coping* (Lazarus & Folkman, 1984) provides guidance in defining and understanding the effects of different ways that people cope with stress. Coping with stress becomes particularly important for pregnant or parenting adolescents as they are challenged with many life changes. The ability to meet life in the present with active coping strategies, acceptance, and perseverance in the face of life difficulties is important.

5. Concepts from Bandura's (2003, 2004) *social learning theory* encourage human agency and self-regulation. This theory provides the basis for the use of multiple incentives and helps adolescents learn how to use external rewards to motivate themselves to do difficult tasks. *Efficacy theory* from this same model (Bandura, 2003, 2004) provides guidance for the intervention's goal of strengthening adolescent mothers' sense of self-efficacy through the mastery of cognitive and behavioral skills.

6. The *social problem solving process* used in the group is based on D'Zurilla and Nezu's (1982) social problem solving model. Adolescent parents, who are just beginning to learn complex problem solving, are often faced with overwhelming problems that need accelerated learning, and this life skill becomes a critical component for their mastery to be successful across the four life domains of education, personal relationships, parenting, and employment/career.

7. The *task-centered group model* (Reid, 1986) provides a structured process to focus on helping the group members to work with other adolescents to tackle current problems in their lives, thereby supporting and enhancing their confidence to master the active problem-solving and coping skills in the day-to-day lives at school, home, and work.

Developmental Framework

The Taking Charge curriculum relies strongly on developmental theory and draws on a developmental framework to intervene with the adolescent mothers. We view human development from a bio-psycho-social-spiritual perspective and believe that human beings are ever striving to grow, adapt, and change in relationship to their life demands. Human development is proactive and by nature resilient in the face of adversity, stress, and change (Greene, 2000). Human cognitive organization is constructed in a way that we are continually using language, cognition, and experience to shape and frame our social realities (Mahoney, 2004). Adolescent pregnancy has been characterized as a maturational or developmental crisis that can create additional stress for the adolescent who has yet to resolve issues of her own personal and social identity (Pines, 1988; Trad, 1994). Pregnancy for the adolescent circumvents the extended process of working through identified developmental tasks. Although adolescent mothers must function in arenas that require adult socialization and skills, they are yet in the process of detaching from childhood and only beginning to establish a separate, adult identity.

Havighurst's (1972) eight developmental tasks for adolescence are compatible with Erickson's stage theory, and were used to think through some of the important developmental life issues facing adolescents and how these issues are impacted by a young woman's pregnancy. We were most concerned with how the following developmental tasks might impact the sense of self-sufficiency of the adolescent mothers across the four life domains that were discussed in chapter 1:

1. Accepting one's physique and using the body effectively

2. Achieving new and more mature relations with age-mates of both genders

3. Achieving a masculine or feminine gender role

4. Achieving emotional independence from parents and other adults

5. Preparing for a career or employment

6. Preparing for marriage and family life

7. Desiring and achieving socially responsible behavior

8. Acquiring a set of values and an ethical system as a guide to behavior—developing an ideology.

It is not difficult to see how each of these eight developmental tasks can be challenged by early pregnancy. Although the eight form an interactive system of developmental process, the four that are most strongly related to strengthening self-sufficiency form the focus for our theoretical frame. The two primary tasks are *preparing for a career or employment* and *preparing for family life*, specifically for the role of parent and provider. The two tasks of *desiring and achieving socially desirable behavior* and *achieving new and more mature relationships with age-mates of both genders* are tasks that support self-sufficiency and parenting. These four themes appear throughout the Taking Charge curriculum.

Related to the developmental tasks of adolescence is the development of role functioning or the ability to achieve a variety of competent interpersonal and social roles. The period of adolescence typically provides a bridge of several years between childhood and adulthood for observing and developing the skills and behaviors required to manage adult roles (Biddle, 1979; Davis, 1996). In fact, those years have been greatly extended in Western societies and continue to lengthen. Adolescent mothers obviously do not get this bridge. Adolescents usually carry several age-prescribed roles, including one set of behaviors as students, another as children or siblings in the family, and another as peers. While engaging actively in these typical roles, the adolescent observes and may begin the early stages of practicing the *role expectations* and *norms* (Davis, 1996) of adult roles such as wage earners (with a part-time job), intimate partners (with dating or a boyfriend), providers (paying for the movies or some of one's own clothing), and parents (babysitting or taking child development classes).

Limited life experience and conflicting developmental tasks may create great stress for the adolescent mother who is thrust into an adult role for which she has not yet developed the skills or social cognition. *Role discontinuity* (Biddle, 1979), the lack of similarity between her adolescent role and her adult role, as well as *role conflict* (Davis, 1996) between her role as adolescent and her adult role as a parent, can be very stressful.

The following is a composite of stories shared by Taking Charge group participants that illustrates such stressful conflict.

Seventeen-year-old Mattie was a junior in high school and the mother of 2-year-old Luke. Mattie and Luke lived with Mattie's mother and younger brother. No longer romantically involved with Luke's father, Mattie was isolated from most of her old friends and devoted herself almost solely to graduating from high school and taking care of her son. She worked at Luke's day care center after school 3 days a week and became friends with a woman on the staff near her age. Mattie's mother agreed to take care of Luke when Mattie's friend invited her to a Saturday evening cookout. Mattie looked forward to the evening out with people her own age. However, on the afternoon of the party, Luke tripped on a rock, resulting in a cut that required several stitches. Mattie went ahead to the party, but she could not stop worrying about Luke and stayed only for a little while. When she arrived home early and found Luke sleeping peacefully, Mattie sat on her bed and cried.

Role discontinuity and role conflict can be even more stressful if the role is seen as deviant or variant, such as that of unmarried mother. "Deviant roles are stigmatized by society, and persons who enact them may internalize a degraded social identity" (Gove, 1975, p. 7). Teen mothers are likely to meet with such social stigma in many areas of their lives, resulting in a sense of inferiority.

The competency of an adolescent mother as a parent and provider is judged by adult standards, in which she is expected to perform capably. The distance between these expectations and traditional expectations for adolescents can add even more stress. New role expectations around parenting and financial provision that she is not prepared to meet can foster overwhelming stress and maladaptive responses.

The Taking Charge curriculum takes into consideration these developmental issues and conflicting role demands by using the four life domains as a foundation for learning and resolving areas of conflict. Further, it reinforces the mother's progress toward normal adolescent developmental tasks, as well as assisting the mother with new life skills that can help her accelerate her learning toward the hastened adult roles.

Solution-Focused Brief Therapy Framework

We designed this curriculum first and foremost to be a strengths-based approach to adolescent motherhood. Research on the life experiences of adolescent mothers supports the fact that despite hardships, adolescent mothers can be resilient and transcend the experiences of early pregnancy and parenthood. They can finish their education, develop meaningful career alternatives, and lead productive lives (Clemmens, 2003). As we progressed in our development of the curriculum, we added solution-focused brief therapy as an anchor for our strengths-based, goal-directed philosophy. We found this type of therapy to be philosophically compatible with the other components of the curriculum. Simply stated, solution-focused brief therapy has the following assumptions that we believe are also consistent with the change philosophy of the curriculum:

1. People can change regardless of their past.

2. People are resilient. Adversity can be positive and a person can change and grow through it.

3. It is important to build on things that are already working with people and what they already know how to do.

4. If something is working well, do not change it ("If it ain't broke, don't fix it").

5. If something is not working well, do something different.

6. Change can be brief and does not have to take a long time.

7. It is more effective to focus on people's strengths than to focus on pathology ("You catch more flies with honey than vinegar").

8. What people say and think are important to what they do, so we must learn to speak the words and think the thoughts that create the futures that we want.

The solution-focused brief therapy is a strengths-oriented intervention with roots in ecological systems theory, social cognitive theory, and social constructionism (e.g., Franklin & Nurius, 1996). This therapy originated in the early 1980s at the Brief Family Therapy Center in

Milwaukee under the leadership of two social workers, Insoo Kim Berg and Steve deShazer. Practitioners have widely applied its techniques in schools (Berg & Shilts, 2005; Franklin, Biever, Moore, Clemons, & Scamardo, 2001; Kral, 1995; Metcalf, 1995; Murphy, 1996; Sklare, 1997; Webb, 1999). As a result, quasi-experimental design studies found that the solution-focused approach has had favorable results with students who have behavioral problems and those who are dropout prone (for a review, see Franklin, Kim, & Tripodi, 2006).

Complementing the developmental framework, the solution-focused brief therapy is a goal-directed therapy that affirms human beings' adaptive and proactive capacities. Goal setting is a very important change strategy in the this type of therapy. The following set of practice guidelines for developing goals in solution-focused brief therapy is adapted from DeJong and Berg (2002, pp. 78–83) and provide useful instructions for how to set workable goals for leaders of the Taking Charge group curriculum:

1. *Goals must be important to the student.* A goal, however, does not have to be something the educational professional thinks is important. In order to elicit cooperation and motivation and build self-confidence and responsibility in people, it is absolutely necessary that goals come from students or clients.

2. *Goals must be described in social interactional terms.* Suppose that you ask an adolescent mom what will be different in her life when her problems are solved. She might say something broad like, "I will feel better, and would not be tired all the time." Solution-focused goal setting would ask this mom to break this broad, general statement down into social and relationship terms. For example, "When you do not feel tired all the time, who would notice that about you? What would be the first small sign to them that you were starting to feel better? What else would they notice? Who else would notice you were feeling better, and what would they say? How would that make you feel?" You would ask for a lot of details about these social interactional perceptions in order to clarify what she wants to change.

3. *Goals must include situational features.* Students are often overwhelmed, discouraged, and fatigued from solving their problems. Sometimes they are just not motivated at the time to put forth huge

efforts to tackle big problems. So, goals are broken down into certain places, times, or settings. For example, a student might tell you that she is having trouble getting to work and school and is in big trouble in both places. The baby has been sick, she has been fighting with her boyfriend, and she has had a lot of personal problems lately. She knows she needs to show up more at both places, but she is currently overwhelmed! Instead of setting a goal to show up every day everywhere she is to be, she might set a goal this week to show up in her math, science, and history classes every day because she is going to fail the entire semester in those subjects if she does not come. She has the option of taking a temporary leave of absence from her work. Her other classes are electives, and she can also more easily make those up. This makes the goal seem more doable. The process of narrowing down goals also makes the process of developing goals seem more possible and provides the needed confidence to move forward.

4. *The presence of desirable behaviors instead of the absence of problems.* It is not unusual for adolescents to describe what they want by what they do not want. They may say, for example, "I do not want my mom to lecture me about the baby. I don't want my boyfriend to hit me. I don't want the teacher to yell at me for being late to school. I have to wait for my aunt to pick up the baby." A goal description like this is rarely useful because it is a negative statement. To become a solution-focused goal statement, it has to become a positive statement. A standard question is, "What would your boyfriend, mother, or teacher being doing instead? What would life look like without the problem?"

5. *A beginning step rather than a final result.* Students often see problems and answers in absolute terms. Either you have the answer, or you don't have the answer. But nothing could be further from the truth. Most issues of life are not solved that way. There are beginning and intermediate steps toward solutions. Goal setting in the solution-focused approach is seen not as an end but as a beginning. The word *goal* is treated as a call to action, as in "Let's go take some steps toward our dreams." Later in this chapter, we explain how the Taking Charge group curriculum uses task setting from the task-centered approach to work toward a goal. Certainly, small steps and tasks are also an

important part of goal setting in solution-focused brief therapy as well.

6. *Clients' recognition of a role for themselves.* Adolescent mothers may feel powerless to do anything about their life problems. They believe that the problems are caused by hopeless circumstances or other people. Consequently, the adolescent will want to set a goal that says that other people will need to change or that life will have to be different which may not be possible. The solution-focused approach goes with the young woman's perception but helps her think through what she might do differently and what behaviors she wants to accomplish. For example, the solution-focused counselor might say, "Let's just suppose that your baby was sleeping through the night, what would you do different as a result? What difference would your teacher see in you, for example?"

7. *Concrete, behavioral, and measurable terms.* The solution-focused approach asks clients to describe very specific goals. One way to know whether a goal is concrete and behavioral enough is to ask yourself whether you can describe the task of the goal in terms of who is doing what, when, and how. Also, the goal should be a task that a person can do in a relatively short period of time and can present proof that they have completed it. The Taking Charge group curriculum follows these kinds of principles in its goal-setting activities and borrows detailed instructions on how to so from the task group approach that is described in more detail below.

8. *Realistic terms.* Sometimes adolescents want to set goals that are not realistic. "My boyfriend would break up with his girlfriend, and we would get married and live happily ever after," for example. A realistic goal, however, has to be achievable given the person's current capacities and context in which they live. The solution-focused educator helps adolescents think through whether a goal is realistic, and what consequences that they are really seeking by asking, "What tells you that this could happen?" or "What difference would this make for you and the baby, for example?"

9. *A challenge to the client.* Many adolescent mothers are ashamed of their personal and family problems and may even feel that they imply that there is something wrong with them because they have ended up

with so many personal problems. For this reason, solution-focused therapy views personal problems as normal life challenges that take hard work to manage. This affirms the dignity and worth of the person and places responsibility for change on them. Goals are an opportunity for people to commit themselves toward the hard work needed to manage life's challenging problems.

Importance of Student-Driven Goals and Dreams

Educational and counseling interventions often have professionals selecting the goals for students, whereas solution-focused brief therapy has an important therapeutic technique that the goal be chosen by the student and not the educator. This technique is often called solution building or solution solving, and these terms mean that the student is being enabled or supported to find her own solutions to life's problems. As an empowerment perspective, the solution-focused approach believes that most people can and want to change themselves, and it is important for helpers to cooperate with the student to create a context for change to make change happen (DeJong & Berg, 2002). Students change in the process of trying out new solutions and learning from their choices.

From our research, we provide a case example of how this type of student-driven goal-setting process works with adolescent mothers (see chapter 4) and add further cautions about why it is imperative for the leaders of the Taking Charge group not to select the goals for the adolescents. Instead, the educator encourages exploring alternatives, experimenting with choices, and experiencing the consequences of choices with support and guidance. It is through this process that adolescents are able to take charge and to even accelerate their developmental learning through experiential learning tasks. In other words, they are able to build autonomy and self-confidence and learn new skills like those that might be necessary in learning to be a parent, managing school, and resolving conflicts with the baby's father.

Using this type of self-directed, experiential learning process, the solution-focused approach builds on human resiliency and the developmental drive to adapt and to learn, to want to move forward and to obtain goals and dreams. Young people strongly believe in their dreams, even when they do not know how to articulate them. The Taking Charge curriculum is designed to build on this developmental reality and offers structured exercises to help adolescent mothers express and set goals toward their life dreams. Because young people do not have a lot of life experiences to draw on, almost everything in life is a new experience for them. Therefore, they are always trying out new behavioral territory and, aside from drawing on the life experiences of those with similar experiences and skills, are on a perpetual learning curve. Of course, as was discussed above, this is quadrupled for adolescent mothers who have entered the fast lane of life development at the same time they are trying to figure out themselves and their dreams. For some adolescent women, having their baby may even be a part of their life dreams but this does not forgo the hardships involved in living out that dream at this stage of their development.

Goal setting is a core component of the solution-focused approach and is facilitative to learning new skills and acquiring life dreams. Goal setting helps adolescents both figure out their dreams and reach their dreams. If educators or other adults, however, are too authority driven and support adolescents too much in the process of discovering goals, this may provoke dependency, rebellion, or avoidance instead of cooperation from young women. This results in interpersonal conflict and resistance that may inadvertently slow down learning. When adolescent women become too dependent, they may not become self-sufficient and may end up relying on others instead of being able to provide for themselves. If they become avoidant in response to harsh authority, they may seem cooperative but lie or miss appointments and never seem to able to follow through with the goals set, resulting in ultimate lack of progress toward their goals. Rebellion leads to lack of cooperation toward goal setting, passive aggression, hostility, and outright aggression toward others. This often leads to lives that sabotage self-sufficiency.

On the opposite end, if there is no authority and guidance, educators and other adults may encounter adolescent women who do not know how to respect rules and consequences, and therefore have to go through an excessive amount of hard knocks before they learn. This can also hinder or prevent self-sufficiency. These women may be antisocial and rebellious, or asocial and alienated, or simply be absent and disconnected from school. Recall that becoming disconnected from school is one of the greatest risks of adolescent pregnancy, as we discussed in chapter 1.

Solution-focused goal setting provides positive feedback and helps adolescent women learn through their own experiences. A delicate combination of respect and honoring the goals and experiences of the adolescent mothers, coupled with consistent positive feedback, is believed to provide the facilitative conditions for the best cooperation and the quickest learning of new behaviors and skills to meet life's toughest challenges. The Taking Charge group curriculum uses this same strengths-based philosophy to set goals with the adolescent mothers across the four life domains that were discussed in chapter 1. For example, adolescent mothers are treated with respect, like adults, and are encouraged to set their own goals across the four life domains of education, personal relationships, parenting and employment/career. When they take the small steps toward their goals, they are complimented and are given all the credit. This supports their self-confidence in that activity and the social and interpersonal competence that is also consistent with developmental tasks.

Problem Solving and the Solution-Building Process

Some writers (e.g., DeJong & Berg, 2002) have drawn sharp distinctions between solution-building techniques and the process and techniques of some forms of problem solving, but we do not see incompatible degrees of differences between the social problem-solving process (to be described in more detail below) that we are using in the Taking Charge group curriculum and the solution-building approach. Therefore, we combine these methods. In order to further support strengths and resources in adolescent mothers, the Taking Charge group curriculum encourages educators to follow this solution-building technique when adolescents identify problems. Adolescents should come up with their own solution. That means that the educator asks questions and encourages the adolescent to use the problem-solving skills that are taught in the group (to be described below and in detail in chapters 3 and 4), but it is up to the student to come up with her own solution to try out.

This is important to the developmental process of adolescents and to the strengths-building process of the Taking Charge group curriculum. Ways to support the adolescent in the problem solving process are illustrated in more detail in chapter 4.

What You Say Is What You Get

The strengths-based, solution-focused approach does not believe that it is very productive to talk about the past problems or anything negative unless it somehow moves the person forward toward his or her goals. So, when a mother talks about problems across the life domains, the educational professional should be thinking about how to help the young woman turn these issues into something constructive for herself, and how to assist her with goals to move beyond these problems. The problem-solving skills intervention taught in the Taking Charge groups offers a systematic way to make this happen (see chapters 3 and 4).

From the solution-focused perspective, however, this work is done through language because through the power of language is the social and the cognitive power to construct cognition, meaning, and beliefs. You may have seen the commercial with the tagline, "Got milk?" Well, the solution-focused therapy asks, "Got words?" People often believe, for example, what they hear themselves say about themselves. Rehearsing problems over and over in your mind and with others in conversations often has an unintended negative outcome. Even more powerful, what we hear other people say about us may shape us, even when it is not true. Other people also may believe what they hear about others and may repeat it to others who say it, and that is why gossip and slander is so damaging. How do you think it affects someone to be described as a *problem child*, for example? What about the description *slut*? The negative things people say about us may become some of the most powerful influences in our lives and no one is exempt from that process.

Of course, language can be used in the opposite way to build people up and affirm them, as every good teacher knows, and the solution-focused approach chooses to use language in this way to introduce new possibilities for thinking and behaving. Integrating this strengths-based philosophy, the Taking Charge group curriculum encourages adolescent mothers to put the past behind them and to focus on the present and the future, to speak positive words about themselves and their potential. Mothers may be asked, for example, to identify their personal assets and to keep a folder about their strengths. Adolescents further try out and explore new behaviors as a way to solve problems across the four life domains. We believe that this strengths-based framework is an especially appropriate and powerful approach for adolescent mothers because, as we discussed previously, pregnant and parenting adolescents are plagued with stigma, discrimination, and a sense of social and moral failure. This approach gives them an opportunity to view themselves and their lives from a totally different, strengths perspective.

Social Learning and Cognitive-Behavioral Theories

Social learning and cognitive-behavioral theories were used to shape the Taking Charge curriculum, especially its life skills interventions of active, social problem-solving and coping-skills training. Social-cognitive and social learning theories, however, are believed to be the guiding theoretical constructs and provide the theoretical and empirical background behind the entire curriculum, including its developmental and strengths-based, solution-focused frameworks that were described previously. In the next sections of this chapter, we will describe how social learning theory and cognitive-behavioral interventions have shaped the Taking Charge group curriculum and why we were convinced that these interventions would be effective with adolescent mothers.

First, social learning and cognitive-behavioral skills approaches focus on the development of new behavior and skills and, as pointed out earlier, this is a monumental task for adolescent mothers: the learning of new roles and behaviors. In fact, as we suggested, accelerated learning is required. We believe the learning technologies inherent in cognitive and social learning skills training approaches show promise for this challenge. Common to all social learning and cognitive-behavioral skills-based approaches with adolescents is a set of four specific steps that have been found to be highly effective in the acquisition of new skills:

(1) practitioner models the skills, (2) client role plays and practices skills in session, (3) client completes homework assignments to continue practicing the skills in her daily life, and (4) practitioner gains feedback from client about her success in learning the skills and adjusts the training to accommodate individual differences that may be encountered in learning. Cognitive and social learning programs also offer a lot of guidance about how to structure learning programs to get the best results, and we believed that the evidence base of these learning technologies could be helpful to accelerating a learning program with adolescent mothers.

Skills training programs, for example, are most effective when they promote a sense of social support, social competence, and self-efficacy (Hogue & Liddle, 1999). Self-monitoring of behavior, point systems, and positive reinforcement for incremental behavior change (i.e., rewards for small steps) are also a part of successful programs. Every indication from research suggests that adolescent mothers would benefit from this type of supportive learning program, so we endeavored to put these types of components into the Taking Charge curriculum. We reasoned that there was already ample evidence that training programs that provide real-world skills practice are the most efficacious in pregnancy prevention, for example. Role playing and in-session, task-related work and homework assignments also appear to be effective tools for learning, as well as group-based peer support and positive reinforcement for the social and life skills being learned. The Taking Charge curriculum therefore included all these learning interventions.

Much of the theoretical origins of cognitive-behavioral skills training interventions may be traced to social learning theory (Bandura, 1999) and the transactional coping theory and problem-solving models developed by Lazarus and Folkman (1984; D'Zurilla & Nezu, 1982). Transactional coping theory and problem-solving theory are the basis for the life skills that are taught in the curriculum. The theoretical basis for both transactional coping and problem solving as effective interventions for adolescent mothers are described in more detail below, but first we will discuss the importance of Bandura's (1999) social learning theory. This theory provides the important theoretical and empirical basis for much of the Taking Charge intervention, including practicing and mastering skills, modeling, and incentive strategies.

Social Learning Theory

Human agency is an important idea in social learning theory. Human agency refers to people having the personal cognitive powers to influence their own actions to produce certain results (Bandura, 1986). Further, the capacity to exercise control over one's thought processes, motivation, affect, and actions is a mechanism of personal agency. An assumption of social learning theory is that we contribute to the formation of the environments we experience (actual environment) and have self-regulatory capability—that is, the ability to observe, judge, and direct our own lives instead of being totally dictated by environmental circumstances (Bandura, 1999). Beyond theories that explain human behavior in terms of environmental influences or internal forces (e.g., Erikson, 1968; Freud, 1905/1953; Pinderhughes, 1988), social learning theory explains our behavior through *triadic reciprocal causation* (Bandura, 1986) between three forces: personal (cognitive, affective, and biological), behavioral, and environmental. The contributions of each of these three depend on the activities, circumstances, constraints, and opportunities imposed by all three.

The capabilities of forethought and self-regulation in the context of triadic reciprocal causality (Bandura, 1999) explain why we incorporated incentives into the curriculum. We anticipated, for example, that participants can conceptualize the satisfaction of receiving lunches, gifts, and awards, and that they can self-regulate their behavior toward ensuring that they will receive these external benefits. Attending school every day, doing homework and extra credit assignments, and performing other self-identified tasks are not behaviors that we expect Taking Charge participants to particularly enjoy, at least initially. Considering the time and energy required, as well as the difficulty of the required behaviors, their immediate environmental feedback may not be enough to sustain self-motivation until the new life skills are learned.

For many adolescent mothers, external incentives are helpful in shoring up self-motivation, especially when temporary setbacks happen. Additionally, the incentives provide an attainable way for group participants to experience the personal satisfaction of earning tangible rewards that come from their own efforts, a valuable way to motivate and reward oneself for sustained effort. Mothers may gain the benefit of learning what most successful people take for granted. Achievement can be rewarding, and we can use external rewards to motivate us to take smaller steps toward sustaining the unpleasant hard work needed toward our achievements. We explain the use of the rewards and point system more in chapters 3 and 4.

Social learning theory suggests that adolescents have much more personal influence to set up their own external influences, because there is a major difference between the *potential* environment and the *actual* environment that we experience. For example, the part of the potential environment that becomes the actual environment depends on how we behave and what we decide. Our choice of relationships, activities, and surroundings constitute our *selected* environment. Our environment and circumstances do not simply exist while we fall helpless like victims to our unfortunate surroundings. We can take control of our thinking and actions, choose our personal relationships and activities, and take charge of our lives!

It is important to mention here, though, that sometimes learning to take control also means learning to accept what we cannot change, and that acceptance strategy offers its own type of personal empowerment, as well, so that we do not wear ourselves out or beat ourselves over the head trying to master things or change things that cannot be affected. We discussed this briefly in chapter 1 in relationship to the adolescent mother's immediate employability, but it is worth repeating here because we are emphasizing self-control and taking charge of our life circumstances.

Self-Efficacy Theory and Taking Charge

The idea that we can self-regulate and take control of our lives is related to Bandura's research on the concept of *self-efficacy*. Self-efficacy is defined as "beliefs of people about their capabilities to exercise control over their own level of functioning and over events that affect their lives" (Bandura, 1991, p. 257). If you will recall our discussion in chapter 1 about the importance of adolescent mothers being able take charge of the risk factors across the four critical life domains regardless of their circumstances, you can grasp the vast importance of these ideas for adolescent mothers.

Efficacy theory assumes that an individual's belief in her own efficacy influences her hopes and goals, how much effort she puts into a given each life domain, and how long she perseveres in the face of difficulties and setbacks. The more capable a mother judges herself to be, the higher the goals she may set for herself and the more firmly committed she remains to them, for example (Bandura, 1991a; Locke & Latham, 1990; Wood & Bandura, 1989). Efficacy also influences whether one's thought patterns are self-hindering or self-aiding. Adolescents who sees themselves as highly effective tend to see their failures as due to insufficient effort, whereas those who see themselves as ineffective view the cause of their failures as evidence of their low ability (Bandura, 1991a; Silver, Mitchell, & Gist, 1989).

Research suggests that self-efficacy impacts outcome in a number of areas that have potential importance for adolescent mothers' behavioral change and resiliency. For example, a sense of personal efficacy has been found to be an important personal resource in human adaptation to stressful life transitions (Jerusalem & Mittag, 1995). It impacts children's and adolescents' scholastic success and vocational interests (e.g., Betz & Hackett, 1981; Lent, Brown, & Larkins, 1987; Zimmerman & Martinez-Ponds, 1990). Self-efficacy also has a strong relationship with the use of problem-focused coping and adjustment (Bandura, 1992; Passino et al., 1993; Stern & Alvarez, 1992). We strongly believe that research supports the importance of strengthening the self-efficacy of adolescent mothers, and we designed the Taking Charge curriculum from a strengths and resiliency perspective with this in mind. We also drew heavily on the work of social learning theory in designing the curriculum because we believe that it has potential to strengthen the self-efficacy of the mothers across the four life domains.

Bandura (1995) identifies four ways to strengthen efficacy beliefs in people:

1. *Mastery* is the most authentic and influential source. This can be achieved by reaching goals or overcoming obstacles in successive attainable steps or small tasks. Successes build a robust belief in one's personal efficacy. Failures undermine it, especially when failures occur before a sense of efficacy is firmly established. Also, when people have only easy successes, they are more quickly discouraged

by failure or setbacks. Bandura (1995) presents the development of resilient self-efficacy as requiring experiences in overcoming obstacles through perseverant effort. In this sense, self-efficacy and problem-focused coping have a circular relationship, in that each is dependent on the other. Mastery experiences, requiring task-centered coping behavior, are essential to self-efficacy, and some degree of self-efficacy is a prerequisite to active coping behavior required for mastery. In other words, setting a challenging goal, working hard toward it, and enduring hardships to obtain the goal are important to a sense of efficacy and mastery. We discussed previously the importance of facilitating adolescents to be able to do this for themselves in relationship to our strengths-based, solution-focused framework and that this is important to mastery and developmental learning for adolescents.

2. *Vicarious experiences provided by social models* is the second source of self-efficacy. "Seeing people similar to themselves succeed by perseverant effort raises observers' beliefs that they, too, possess the capabilities to master comparable activities" (Bandura, 1995, p. 3). The impact of modeling on beliefs of personal efficacy is strongly influenced by perceived similarity to the model. The greater the assumed similarity, the more persuasive are the model's successes and failures. We found that it was important to include some successful teen moms in the program when possible, even as a coleader, and to make use, as much as possible, of successful personal testimonies of the young women about how they had overcome obstacles. Including successful personal testimonies tends to be a highly effective technique.

3. *Social persuasion* is the third source. When individuals are persuaded verbally that they have the abilities to master given activities, they are more likely to muster greater effort and persevere than when they have self-doubts and dwell on personal deficiencies when problems arise (Bandura, 1999). To the degree that persuasive boosts in perceived self-efficacy lead people to try hard enough to succeed (experience mastery), self-affirming persuasion promotes development of skills and a sense of personal efficacy. However, unrealistic boosts in efficacy lose their impact when efforts are disappointing and unsuccessful. Social persuaders need to do more than convey faith in people's capabilities. They need to encourage and guide activities (tasks) in ways that bring success. Social persuasion is most

effective when coupled with structured opportunity for mastery experiences.

Borrowing from the solution-focused approach, we used the ideas of social persuasion through amplifying positive behaviors and focusing on strengths. It requires providing structured activities and tasks that are designed by the adolescents and then following up with compliments, support, encouragement, and getting the details of every successful step, being impressed, and so forth. The structure we put around this process came from the task-centered group process, to be described below and more in chapters 3 and 4.

4. *The individual's own physiological and emotional state in judging their capabilities* is the fourth source. Stress reactions and tension can be interpreted as signs of vulnerability to poor performance. Fatigue, aches, and pains are seen as signs of physical debility. Positive mood enhances perceived self-efficacy, whereas despondency diminishes it. "Thus the fourth way of altering efficacy beliefs is to enhance physical status, reduce negative emotional states, and correct misinterpretations of somatic sources of information" (Bandura, 1999). Active, social problem solving and coping has the advantage of helping adolescents learn to evaluate emotional states and how changing moods might interfere with active problem solving. Adolescents have a chance to evaluate the fact that feelings are fickle! Emotions are more unpredictable than the weather. Feelings are unreliable, and we must not be guided solely by them. Instead, Taking Charge urges adolescent women to make goals their guides and helps the adolescents to think through some of their emotional issues that might impact their mastery of the problem-focused coping taught in the curriculum.

Transactional Coping Theory

According to the transactional theory of stress and coping, how grave and troublesome an adolescent's stress symptoms are is determined by her *appraisal* of a situation or event. She can see it as presenting personal harm or loss, a threat, or a challenge (Lazarus & Folkman, 1984).

- *Harm or loss* refers to appraisal in which the person has already sustained some damage, such as an injury or illness, damage to social esteem, or loss of a loved or valued person.

- *Threat* concerns appraisal of harms or losses that have not yet happened but are expected. The significance of threat is that it allows *anticipatory coping*. To the extent that the individual can anticipate the future, she can plan for it and work through some of the anticipated problems in advance.

- *Challenge* is similar to loss and threat in that it also calls for mobilizing coping efforts. The main difference is that challenge appraisal focuses on possible gain or growth from the encounter and is accompanied by pleasurable emotions such as excitement, hope, and eagerness.

Coping is a response to losses, threats, or challenges, and how we cope depends on our appraisal. This is a complex process that involves personality characteristics, personal relationships, and situational parameters (Pierce, Saranson, & Saranson, 1996). Early in the development of coping theory, Lazarus and Launier (1978) defined two broad categories of coping: direct actions and palliative modes. *Direct actions* were seen as responses designed to alleviate the problem or threat. *Palliative modes* referred to relieving the emotional impact of the problem through activities such as meditation or physical exercise. Endler and Parker (1990) broke these into three ways that categorize the way most people deal with problems or stress:

1. *Action-focused coping*, also termed *problem-focused coping*, refers to active efforts to change the external situation, such as forming and carrying out a plan of action.

2. *Emotion-focused coping*, the second dimension, refers to attempts to change one's thinking and emotional responses without directly influencing the external situation, such as focusing on what good can come of the event.

3. *Avoidance* is the strategy of avoiding or trying not to think of the event, frequently using other activities as distractions.

The type of coping people use logically explains differences in their outcomes, even when their problems are basically the same. In fact, research shows a stronger connection between coping and the outcome than between the extent of the problem and the outcome (Zeidner & Hammer, 1990). This suggests that our *method* of coping with problems may be more important to our outcome than the frequency and severity of our problems. Previous studies tell us that people who use problem-focused coping more often than emotion-focused or avoidant coping have more successful outcomes (Passino et al., 1993; Stern & Alvarez, 1992).

From these observations, we concluded that strengthening the use of problem-focused coping should be included in a curriculum designed to help young mothers toward self-sufficiency. Studies on coping responses have found this theory relevant to several issues associated with adolescent pregnancy. One of these is overall adjustment. A number of studies done on adolescent mothers focus on stress and coping theory with the issue of adjustment (e.g., Barth & Schinke, 1984; Passino et al., 1993; Stern & Alvarez, 1992). They indicate that adolescents in general use a variety of coping responses, ranging from problem-focused and active to passive or emotion-focused strategies (Stern & Alvarez, 1992; Stern & Zevon, 1990; Tolor & Fehon, 1987). This applies particularly to stressors associated with parenthood (Colletta & Gregg, 1981; Unger & Wandersman, 1988). For example, a tendency to avoid or passively adjust to problems rather than make active attempts to resolve problems has been found in pregnant and parenting adolescents to a greater degree than in nonpregnant/parenting adolescents (Codega, Pasley, & Kreutzer, 1990). Research suggests that persons who use active problem-focused strategies adjust more successfully than those who use passive strategies (de Anda, 1998; Wege & Moller, 1995).

Radical Acceptance and Problem-Focused Coping

Problem-focused coping, in which people engage and actively try to do something about their situation, gets better results than passivity or avoidance, and research supports this approach with pregnant and parenting adolescents. Other research on cognitive-behavioral change interventions also tells us, however, that radical acceptance strategies are also important to behavioral change and problem solving in the face of great difficulties. Radical acceptance differs from more active change strategies like problem-focused coping because the person has to give up trying to actively control and influence the immediate outcome of the problem. Radically acceptance, however, does not imply passivity, avoidance, or resignation to life problems but rather to be able to embrace whatever is in the present moment without a sense of emotional attachment or demands for immediate gratification or change (Robins, Schmidt, & Linehan, 2004).

Too often people are blocked from success in school and other areas because they are unable to accept life as it is in the present and persevere without letting themselves to get too emotionally upset or discouraged about it. Their prior learning history, emotional attachments, beliefs, and expectations prompt them to hold on to the past or give up on the future. "I think I ruined my life by getting pregnant when I was 15. Just like my auntie said, 'There is no getting over it,'" for example. This young woman obviously cannot change the fact that she got pregnant at 15. No active problem focused, change strategy will change that fact. What is needed is a different kind of problem-solving method that allows her to persist through this circumstance and to change her thinking about it.

That is where radical acceptance comes in. Research suggests that in order to succeed in the face of adversity and stress that we must develop cognitive flexibility, the abilities to explore, change, and to continually challenge our own thinking and perceptions, even our very words and emotional cues about what is happening. (Hayes, Follette, & Linehan, 2004). In order to move past where she is with her pregnancy, this young woman will need this type of learning and coping skills. It is important for her to be able to be flexible enough to actively problem solve but to also be able to accept and persevere through the tough times when the circumstances will not budge.

When adolescent mothers develop both active coping strategies and radical acceptance skills, they will be better prepared to handle what John Gottman (1999) discovered in his family relationship research and called "perpetual problems." A "perpetual problem" is that set of issues in life about ourselves and others that do not completely go away through active problem solving or other active efforts at resolution. A "perpetual problem" persists with us, and we have to continually find ways to cope and problem solve through the issues. This might require a combination of active problem solving and persisting on through the hard times, while not letting your emotional upsets about the fact that the problems continue interfere with your progress in life. It is an on-going process.

Some of the challenges of adolescent pregnancy and parenting, for example, may fall in the category of being a "perpetual problem" (e.g., baby's father, disabled child, difficult mother-in-law, and you can probably think of a few). We illustrate this with a proverb, "you cannot unscramble eggs." If a teenage mom sits around sullen, sad, and defeated because she wanted eggs that were poached instead of scrambled, she will go hungry. To nurture herself, she must learn ways to accept the scrambled eggs, eat her breakfast, and get on with her day.

We designed the Taking Charge group curriculum to be strongly change-focused because the research supports this problem-focused coping approach with adolescent mothers. We are also aware that recent experimental research has supported radical acceptance strategies as important to cognitive-behavioral interventions as much as active change strategies, and may even improve outcomes (see Hayes, Follette, & Linehan, 2004, for a review). Our clinical experience with adolescent mothers also confirms that integrating the methods of radical acceptance will be helpful with the mothers. For this reason, in the group process we also encourage leading adolescents in a learning process that helps them accept the reality of their present situation, and focuses them on persevering through it. This therapeutic process is easily incorporated into the task-centered group process that is discussed below. This process focuses young women on the reality of their life situation and helps them to gain the practice they need in order to apply problem-focused coping strategies.

Viewing Is Doing

Whether we are able to accept our problems and persevere or use a problem-focused coping strategy has a lot to do with how we appraise or judge a problem. That is, if we judge a problem situation or event as something that we can change to our advantage, we are more likely to use problem-focused coping strategies than if we judge the problem as one that is beyond our ability to affect. This assumption is supported in a study by MacNair and Elliott (1992), which found that as people's perceptions of their coping effectiveness increase, they are more likely to "tackle the problem" by using problem-focused coping. We can conclude, then, that judging or appraising a problem with a strong sense of confidence or self-efficacy is more likely to inspire us to engage in problem-focused or active coping rather than in avoidant or passive coping.

This all suggests that when adolescent mothers reduce the sense of threat or challenge that they attach to a problem and concurrently have greater confidence in their coping skills, their active coping will increase. This goes right along with the ideas behind radical acceptance strategies for behavioral change that we were discussing above because the problem is no longer given the meaning to exert so much influence and power over our lives. The problem is the problem, and we can observe it in the present as being separate from self in a detached and nonemotional way.

We believe that this approach may even facilitate a more conscious level of problem solving and self-awareness. When we are not emotionally upset about something or too attached to it or trying to control the outcome of an interaction, we can often think more clearly about our surroundings and circumstances, for example. From these ideas, however, two essential components for training come to mind: (1) helping the adolescent to believe that she is capable and that the threat or challenge can be altered or managed by using identified strategies and (2) helping her believe that she herself can successfully carry out the identified strategy.

We hoped to achieve a strategy for developing a type of conscious, social problem-solving training in our work with the young women in the groups. The typical problem-solving mechanisms of adolescents are likely to be inadequate for confronting the complex problems related to becoming parents and providers. Enhancing problem-solving skills, therefore, is important in increasing the frequency with which young mothers use problem-focused rather than passive or avoidant coping mechanisms. The model used in the Taking Charge group curriculum, developed as a clinical tool for applying transactional coping theory (D'Zurilla & Nezu, 1982), provides a compatible structure for teaching and practicing effective social problem-solving skills with young mothers.

Social Problem-Solving Skills

Our objective for an intervention that seeks to strengthen problem-focused coping is to increase skills that most strongly enforce problem-focused coping. We believe that social problem solving is a primary skill to enhance problem-focused behavior. A related benefit is that skill *mastery,* the source of self-efficacy that Bandura (2003) describes as most powerful, is also likely to be positively impacted by enhancing problem-solving skills. We also believed that it was important to use solution building (the mothers were supported to find their own goals and solutions) and to focus on strengths and resources of the mothers, thus enhancing their sense of problem solving and mastery across the four critical life domains of education, personal relationships, parenting, and employment/career. We believe that by following this approach, it is possible to accelerate the learning and rapid development needed to help young mothers to become self-sufficient.

The problem-solving process used in the Taking Charge group curriculum is based on D'Zurilla's and Nezu's (1982) social problem-solving model. Developed as a clinical application of transactional coping theory, this problem-solving process was initially used with depressed individuals. It has since been found effective with other issues such as anxiety, weight loss, delinquent behavior, and academic achievement (e.g., Black, 1987; Cormier, Otani, & Cormier, 1986; D'Zurilla & Sheedy, 1992; Wege & Moller, 1995).

In this approach to problem solving, a *problem* is a life situation that requires a response for effective or adaptive functioning, but for which no effective or adaptive response is immediately apparent or available to the individual. *Social problem solving* is defined as a cognitive-behavioral process through which a person attempts to identify effective means of coping with problems encountered in everyday living (D'Zurilla & Nezu, 1982).

In the Taking Charge group, the social problem-solving process (D'Zurilla & Nezu, 1982) includes four problem-solving skills described as *goal-directed tasks*, which essentially make up the social problem-solving process. These tasks or skills are identified thus:

1. Problem definition and formulation
2. Generation of alternative solutions
3. Decision making/goal setting
4. Solution implementation and verification

The goal of *problem definition and formulation* is to identify and clarify the nature of the problem, including its consequences and who/what is involved. The goal of *generating alternative solutions* is to identify or create as many solution alternatives as possible, assuming that the best possible solution will be among them. In *decision making/goal setting,* the objective is to compare the possible solutions and choose the best as the primary goal for solving the problem. The purpose of *solution implementation and verification* is to carry out tasks needed to accomplish the chosen goal, and to self-monitor the process and evaluate the actual outcome.

It is very important to keep in mind that it is the adolescent mothers who must learn to work their way through these steps and choose the best solution as their primary goal for solving the problem. As was pointed out previously, when we were discussing the strengths-based, solution-focused framework and goal setting, it is counterproductive for adult leaders to assume this role and select the goal for the adolescent. We believe that in order for the problem-solving, skills-building intervention to be effective at moving the adolescents toward mastery and self-sufficiency across the four life domains, the adolescent mothers must fully embrace and be in charge of their own goals and solutions. Even when it is necessary for other people to directly assist them or for them to receive outside resources, the adolescent mothers must actively participate in the goals and the steps toward the obtainment of the resources. This helps the mothers gain confidence in applying the problem solving skills and maintain a sense of empowerment over their circumstances needed to develop a sense of mastery and self-efficacy. We believe this approach is consistent with the social cognitive theory and has the best opportunity to lead to the development of a self-sufficient lifestyle. The steps of problem solving and techniques for how to let the adolescents select their own goals and solutions are illustrated further with case examples in chapter 4.

Taking Charge Structure and Modality

Peer relationships are dominant in the social needs of adolescents. In achieving emotional independence from parents and other adults, adolescents turn to peers for reflection and processing thoughts and behaviors. Friendships appear to become more stable, intimate, and mutually responsive in adolescence (Gegas & Seff, 1990; Richmond, Rosenfeld, & Bowen, 1998), and adolescents' friendships are based within their peer group (e.g., Savin-Williams & Berndt, 1990). Particularly by middle adolescence, peers become equal to parents as providers of emotional nurturance and surpass parents as a source of intimacy and companionship (Hunter & Youniss, 1982). Peer friendships in adolescence have also been found to facilitate the development of social skills such as mutual understanding, role taking, and empathy (Gegas & Seff, 1990; Savin-Williams & Berndt, 1990). In response to the importance of peer interaction and support for achieving skills and socialization, Taking Charge operates in a group modality.

Group Modality

Group intervention as a modality for adolescents is heavily endorsed throughout social work, counseling, and educational practice (e.g., Dupper, 1998; Franklin, McNeil, & Wright, 1991; Nadelman, 1994; Rice & Meyer, 1994). The mutual support process known as *mutual aid,* inherent to groups (Gitterman & Shulman, 1994), has been shown especially effective with adolescents (Nadelman, 1994). Numerous social factors as well as clinical advantages have been identified that support the use of groups for adolescent intervention, as seen in box 2.2.

Box 2.2   **Advantages of Group Intervention With Adolescents**

*Social Advantages to Group
Intervention*

- Adolescents accept feedback more readily from peers than from adults.

- Groups emphasize peer interactions and the importance of personal relationships.

- Group norms are powerfully socializing.

- Members benefit vicariously from work done by others in the group.

- Groups provide an opportunity to listen without demanding immediate participation.

*Clinical Advantages to Group
Intervention*

- The relief of pressure for constant, obvious participation helps to alleviate the silent resistance that is often present in individual work with adolescents (Glodich & Allen, 1998).

- Groups support experimentation with functional, long-term change. Interpersonal relating styles, values about relationships and life goals, and general behavior can be observed and evaluated through the process of feedback.

- Feelings of isolation and being different can be reduced. Group participants have the opportunity to develop peer support and learn to rely on peers, which is a substantial need identified in studies with pregnant and parenting adolescents

Sources: de Anda & Becerra (1984); de Anda et al. (1992); Kymissis (1993).

The Task-Centered Group Model

The task-centered group model of social work structures the Taking Charge group curriculum with a format and process that supports anticipated results. It provides a forum for focusing on strengths, learning and practicing social problem-solving skills, strengthening self-efficacy through mastery, participating in vicarious experiences, learning from social persuasion and corrective self-interpretations, and enhancing task-focused coping behavior through the performance of tasks and behaviors between sessions (Reid, 2001; Reid & Fortune, 2006).

The task-centered group model is a form of short-term, goal-oriented treatment appropriate for individuals, families, and groups. The model was first tested in the 1960s at the Community Service Society of New York. Results suggested that brief psychosocial intervention might provide a more efficient means of helping individuals and families with problems than conventional, long-term forms of psychosocial practice (Reid, 1996, 2001). In its initial development, the task-centered approach used a time-limited structure and short-term psychosocial casework techniques to help clients develop and carry out actions or tasks to alleviate their problems.

Studies of groups with mental health disorders, families dealing with attempted suicide, marital couples, children with academic problems, and adolescents in residential treatment and in academic settings have reported that the task-centered approach is highly effective. One appeal of a task-centered group intervention with adolescent mothers is that it is consistent with our developmental and strengths-based, solution-focused framework and does not assume pathology. The theoretical base of the model focuses primarily on psychosocial problems, on alleviating client-identified problems through actions (tasks) carried out between sessions by the group participant (Fortune, 1985). Some well-known targets of the model are social roles, decision making, securing resources, and emotional distress reactive to situational factors (Reid, 1996). These issues are relevant for the risk factors we have identified across the four critical life domains and are highly relevant for adolescent mothers and the Taking Charge group curriculum.

The time-limited aspect of task-centered work is another feature that makes it especially useful with pregnant and parenting adolescents. "The planned brevity of the model is based on the proposition that effectiveness of interpersonal treatment is relatively short-lived; that is, the most benefit clients will get from such treatment will be derived within relatively few sessions and a relatively brief period of time" (Reid, 1996, p. 620). Evidence suggests that recipients of brief, time-limited treatment show at least as much long-term improvement as those receiving long-term, open-ended treatment. Studies show that most of the client changes previously associated with long-term treatment actually happen relatively soon after treatment begins (Bloom, 1992). In fact, most courses of voluntary treatment span no more than a dozen sessions—

suggesting that most people gain the benefits of treatment fairly early in the process (Garfield, 1994; Koss & Shiang, 2002).

Other features of the task-centered group approach are highly consistent with our strengths-based, solution-focused framework and the social problem-solving process. First, there is a *focus on the present and the future*. Second, the task-centered model stresses *goal setting and the individual's own problem-solving abilities* to negotiate and carry through with actions to obtain what she wants. Third, from a task-centered perspective, *the adolescent mother is seen as having a mind and a will that are reactive but not bound by her past experiences or environment*. Fourth, *human relationships are important and interpersonal support is seen as creating facilitative conditions for change*. For this reason, the similarity of group members around target problems is important for this model. A task-centered group can be processed best when all group members are familiar with the kind of problems others are experiencing and can engage and benefit from one another's process. Five to 7 members is usually thought to be the ideal for a task-centered group (Garvin, 1986), although the task-centered group can effectively range from 8 to about 12. Considerations such as the members' ages and other characteristics, as well as conditions of the group setting, should determine the number of participants for a group. Two leaders cofacilitating the group are considered ideal with this model, although one facilitator, when necessary, can lead a group.

Fifth, *the task-centered group model uses a series of problem-solving steps that are structured*. These steps set an appropriate framework to teach the active, social problem-solving, and coping skills to the adolescent mothers and to give them the opportunity to select their own solutions as is necessary in our developmental, strengths-based and mastery-based approach. We adapted the following steps that Fortune (1985) developed in three phases as our method to teach the active problem-focused coping skills to the adolescent mothers:

1. *Problem specification.* The focus is on determining the problems the client wishes to work on. This is expected to take place in the first 1–3 sessions. During this phase, a contract is developed, written or verbal, which delineates the problems, goals, and duration of treatment. *Focus is on what the client wants and not on what the practitioner*

thinks the client may need (Reid, 1996). However, the practitioner may engage with the client in a mutual process of deliberation in which the practitioner contributes her or his own knowledge and perception, arriving at an explicit agreement on the identified problems.

2. *Task panning and implementation.* The focus is on formulating, planning, and evaluating tasks to resolve target problems. A task is an action that the participant agrees to take toward resolving the problem. Group leaders and participants define the task in a highly structured way, thus increasing chances that the task will be accomplished (Reid & Epstein, 1972). The model offers specific strategies to assist the participant during this phase of intervention. One of these is assessing whether the group member has the knowledge and skills to perform as she desires, and if not, how to develop them. Another strategy, especially when the problem involves a formal organization, is for the practitioner to act as an advocate on behalf of the client to the organization (Garvin, 1986). Active practitioner involvement as a strategy has evolved as preferable over clinical techniques such as encouragement, direction, and explanation, and it expresses the collaborative spirit of the model—what the practitioner and client do together to achieve common ends (Reid, 1986).

3. *Termination.* Progress is reviewed and summarized, and plans are made to increase lasting results from intervention gains. The last 1 to 2 sessions are assigned to this phase.

Although this structure has become more clearly defined as research on the model has progressed, it is a framework rather than an explicit prescription and should be used flexibly. The problem-solving training model for problem-focused coping (D'Zurilla & Nezu, 1999) overlaps and complements components of the task-centered model and can be used compatibly. This condition of the task-centered model makes it more adaptable to Taking Charge than other brief intervention models.

Forming and Conducting a Task-Centered Group

The process of forming and conducting groups varies in different settings, although the general format is similar. When possible, an individual interview is held with each prospective group member to orient the prospective member to the structure and purpose of the group (Reid, 1986). Studies of this process (Yalom, 1995) demonstrate that members who are prepared in this way for the group experience are more responsive in the group and relate more quickly to the group than those who are not prepared.

In the first group session, participants identify the problems they want to work on and help one another in problem exploration and identification. In subsequent sessions, each member conceives, plans, practices, reviews, and carries out tasks with the help of the leaders and other group members.

These are three effective strategies for preparing adolescents for carrying out tasks that may be unfamiliar or threatening:

1. Have members role-play the situation with leader or other participants.

2. Have group leaders or other participants model behavior.

3. Use actual guided practice, in which the participant carries out the task under the guidance of the leader or the group, rather than simply rehearsing it.

These activities are especially beneficial in a group because of the modeling, as well as the available group support. Role-play and modeling are easy to use this way in the Taking Charge group.

In summary, the task-centered group model is a time-limited, brief series of group sessions that emphasizes helping individuals with specific problems of their own choosing through explicit actions or tasks. The model works well for the Taking Charge group for several reasons:

- Compatibility with our developmental and strengths-based, solution-focused frameworks

- Potential for strengthening coping skills and self-efficacy

- Similarity to the social problem-solving model

- Time-limited and brief process

- Emphasis on current problems and future actions

- Stress on similarity in group participants
- Relatively structured process

Brief Educational Programs for Adolescent Mothers

Funding and organizational constraints limit most programs, especially those in regular school settings, to the last months of pregnancy and a few months following birth. This suggests a need for effective short-term interventions. Seitz and Apfel (1999, cited in Harris & Franklin, 2003) review several research-based programs that are short term and educational, and they cite evidence that these programs produce positive outcomes with adolescent mothers. Programs for adolescent mothers appear to be especially effective when offered at critical developmental opportunities or "teachable moments" such as when the baby is first born and the mother is especially receptive to the support and guidance. According to Seitz and Apfel (1999), effective programs contain these aspects:

- A focus on skills to help adolescent mothers prepare themselves for the challenges of life management, parenting, and work

- Self-selected goals that adolescents want to pursue

- Program goals that may pertain to building capacity for parenting and independent living, and the achievement of self-efficacy in the mothers through helping them to achieve successes in parenting, school, and work

- Programs offered in such a manner that the participants perceive the program as helping them rather than punishing them

- Emphasis on strengths, assets, and skill development rather deficits and shortcomings

- Encouragement of individualized learning goals and relationship support systems

- Programs that are structured, short term, and are offered in schools

- Programs that immediately respond to the concerns of mothers when they first become pregnant/parenting and are still in school, rather than after they have dropped out

All of these program goals are consistent with the multimodal, brief, cognitive-behavioral, group curriculum provided by Taking Charge.

Summary

In this chapter, we explained the theoretical and empirical basis for the Taking Charge group curriculum, a multimodal, brief, cognitive, behavioral curriculum. This intervention was developed within developmental and strengths-based, solution-focused frameworks, utilizing the strengths, resources, life goals, and developmental tasks of adolescent mothers. The curriculum is presented as an 8- to 12-week, school-based intervention offered within a task-centered group.

The chapter summarized the curriculum's developmental and strengths-based, solution-focused frameworks, and the core life skills of active, social problem solving and coping that are taught to accelerate learning across the four life domains. The life skills training used in the curriculum is based on social learning and cognitive-behavioral interventions, and the importance and potential effectiveness of these types of skills with adolescent mothers was discussed. This chapter explained the importance of the task-centered group approach that is used to teach the cognitive-behavioral skills to the adolescent mothers. The task-centered group is a highly structured approach that includes a task-driven, problem solving process, and this approach further shares many of the same assumptions to solution solving as the strengths-based, solution-focused and mastery-based frameworks. Finally, we discussed why we believe that brief, group programs like the Taking Charge are important to the school's programs and can be effective in a school setting.

Chapter 3   *The Taking Charge Practice Training Manual*

This book is a comprehensive leadership, training, and practice guide to organizing and leading the Taking Charge group curriculum. This chapter contains step-by-step guidance instructing leaders on how to facilitate each session of the Taking Charge group. Forms and material needed to facilitate each session are found at the end of the chapter. This chapter serves as a training manual by providing detailed instructions and dialogue for leaders to follow when conducting the groups, in order to assure the best intervention fidelity. It is intended to serve as a leader's guide for each group session. For this chapter to be most effective as a training tool, it should be presented in a training group, where it can best provide practice and clarification opportunities for new leaders. It is not recommend, however, that this chapter be used in leadership training groups until potential leaders have read the entire contents of this book

Taking Charge Group Curriculum Goals

Adolescent mothers who participate in the Taking Charge group will hopefully gain many benefits, but there are three primary outcome goals:

1. To increase the adolescent mother's use of *problem-focused coping* strategies, while decreasing her use of avoidance or passive adaptation to deal with problems across the four critical life domains of education, personal relationships, parenting, and employment/career.

2. To increase the competent use of *social problem-solving skills* across the four critical life domains.

3. To increase an adolescent mother's *school achievement* through improved grades and attendance. School achievement and subsequent graduation is believed to be an adolescent mother's first step toward establishing a life of self-sufficiency.

The reader can find an expanded discussion of problem-focused coping, social problem solving, and school achievement in chapter 4.

Adolescent women who become parents enter the fast lane of human development and need accelerated learning to be able to master many new roles. The learning curve is steep for these young women who are already negotiating the usual identity and developmental changes of adolescence. The challenges of parenthood force them to grow up fast and throw them into a crisis-like state, but fortunately with this state of mind also come an amazing resiliency and openness to learning that we do not experience in any other state of mind. Accelerated learning and rapid developmental change is possible.

It is important to build on the competencies of adolescent mothers constantly affirming their strengths and resources. Techniques such as having mothers set their own goals and solutions helps them build their own developmental competence because they experience success from their own solutions. Leaders should keep in mind that a well-constructed goal: (1) is important to the client, (2) is stated in social interactional terms so you can tell whom the goal is affecting, (3) includes situational features such as time, place, and context, (4) has the presence of desirable behaviors rather than the absence of problems, (5) is viewed as a beginning step rather than a final result, (6) includes a role in which the students assume responsibility for themselves, (7) is stated in specific, behavioral, and measurable terms, (8) is realistic for the students' capacity and current situation, and (9) is perceived as being hard work by the student.

Leaders can further reinforce this success of goal achievement by helping the mothers speak positively about each success, coaching the group to affirm the success in one another, and complimenting the mothers. For this technique to work, every small detail about the success must be noticed and elaborated by the mother herself and the mother must verbally acknowledge her positive outcomes and fully embrace and

Taking Charge

recognize how she made each positive outcome happen by her own efforts.

Problem-Focused Coping

The type of coping that people use in dealing with stress affects their overall life adjustment. In the case of adolescent mothers, adjustment refers to how well they are able to manage their new roles and responsibilities as parents and providers. People who use active coping to deal with problems more often than simply trying to adjust to the problem (emotion-focused coping) or avoid the problem (avoidance coping) are more successful in managing or reducing their problems. Teenagers use a variety of coping responses, from problem-focused to passive strategies. Studies show that passive or avoidant coping is particularly prevalent when adolescents are dealing with problems related to being parents.

Avoiding problems or adjusting to them rather than actively trying to find a resolution is found more often with adolescent mothers than with teens who have never been pregnant. Because research suggests that people who use active strategies for dealing with problems adjust more successfully than those who use passive strategies, active coping is an important life skill for adolescent mothers to develop. Research shows that the ability to meet life in the present with active coping strategies, to accept one's circumstances, and to persevere in the face of life difficulties is important for changing behavior and managing life difficulties.

Social Problem-Solving Skills

When an adolescent is confronted suddenly with the demands of parenthood, a set of new, unpracticed, unintegrated behaviors and skills is required. For perhaps the first time, the pregnant adolescent is without the stored knowledge and practiced resources that may have served well to solve life problems in the past. For the first time, she must learn how to consciously analyze her needs and problems, determine her goals, and devise ways to achieve what she needs. An important goal of this group intervention is for participants to learn a solution-solving process and application of conscious, social problem solving as a current and future life tool.

Self-Efficacy

A sense of personal efficacy—competence—has been found to be an important personal resource in people dealing with stressful life changes. Becoming a parent during adolescence is one of the most stressful transitions anyone can make. Full of demanding first-time experiences and difficulties, it can undermine even the strongest self-confidence. Efficacy theory says that people who have a low sense of efficacy or belief in their own competence in certain areas shy away from difficult tasks, which they see as personal threats. They have weak hope and weak commitment to the goals they choose to pursue. They give up quickly when the going gets rough and are slow to recover their sense of efficacy following failure or a setback.

A strong sense of efficacy, however, helps with accomplishing goals and with a personal sense of well-being. People who believe strongly in their own capabilities set challenging goals and stay strongly committed to them. They quickly recover their sense of confidence and commitment after failures or setbacks. They approach threatening situations believing that they can gain control over them. The most important thing about self-efficacy for the goals of this group is this: *A person's self-efficacy beliefs can change through experience and the kind of deliberate strengths and mastery-based interventions that are built into the Taking Charge group curriculum from start to finish.*

Task-Centered Objectives

The primary path for helping group participants to develop life skills in the three group goals is for the adolescents to perform specific *tasks* toward achieving their own strengths-based, solution-focused, self-selected goals. Refer back to chapter 2 for a description of the solution-focused goal process. Once the group has learned the mechanics of the social problem-solving process, each participant will develop her own goal in each of four critical life domains: school achievement, personal relationships, parenting, and employment/career.

For each goal, group participants will identify at least two tasks that they will perform during the week between group sessions. Performing such tasks helps young mothers to gain experience in new, perhaps intimidating, activities and to achieve some sense of mastery over a broader range of life skills and social interactions. Once some mastery is achieved, or when the young mother is at least getting comfortable with her new behavior, she is more likely to repeat it and incorporate it as a part of her normal coping behavior.

Planning the Taking Charge Group

In this section we discuss specific considerations about time frames and dates in planning a Taking Charge group. As most readers who work in schools already know, these considerations are essential for successfully fitting a group intervention into a busy school environment.

Duration and Times

The group meets every week for either 8 or 12 weeks. Each session should be given at least 60 minutes; 80 minutes is ideal. An important consideration for scheduling the meeting day and time is to know which days participants are most likely to be at school. From prior Taking Charge studies, for example, we learned that Mondays and Fridays are days when absences are highest in many schools. Conversely, young mothers in previous groups reported that as they became engaged with the group, they would often make a special effort to be at school on "group day."

Anyone who works in a school setting knows that it is almost impossible to plan an 8- or 12-week group intervention during a time when there will be no interruptions. Even so, it is important to consider holidays, exams, and other school-related events when scheduling Taking Charge.

This is especially true for the first 4 to 5 sessions, when participants are engaging with the group and struggling with new behaviors and skills.

Extending to 12 Weeks

Although Taking Charge has been studied only as an 8-week group intervention, we have received feedback from participants and leaders who tell us a 12-week intervention may be effective, even desirable. The group can be extended easily to 12 sessions by allowing 2 weeks rather than 1 for each goal domain. Sessions 1, 2, 11, and 12 of a 12-week group are identical to sessions 1, 2, 7, and 8 of an 8-week group. Sessions in which goals and tasks are identified and performed are given 2 weeks for each goal area, rather than 1. In most schools, offering a 12-week group would mean beginning the group immediately at the start of the semester, in order to accommodate for interruptions, and completing the group by semester's end.

Group Session Format

Group sessions are structured to follow a similar format throughout. The following describes activities for the three segments of each session.

- *First 25 minutes:* While participants are eating lunch or snack, leaders engage the group in a discussion. Topics of discussion vary from session to session but may include the problem-solving process, the particular goal domain for the session, or participant experiences with tasks between sessions.

- *Next 30–40 minutes:* With the exception of the first two sessions, the group remains together or divides into two groups designated by the leaders. During this time, participants work the problem-solving process, beginning with identifying their goal and ending with two specific tasks that they plan to perform before the next session.

- *Final 10–15 minutes:* Leaders respond to concerns and questions, present points-earned reports, summarize the session, and identify topics and activities for the next session. At 2 sessions (3 sessions in a 12-session intervention), small incentive gifts are presented during this time.

Guide to Facilitating Sessions 1 Through 8

The following section provides a detailed guide to facilitating each Taking Charge group session. It includes leader instructions and dialogue, group activities, handouts, and forms that participants and leaders will use in the group.

Designating Leader Roles

Group leaders should designate as *Leader 1* or *Leader 2* for the purpose of following treatment manual instructions. Treatment manual directions assume that Leader 1 is on the school staff or is someone who has day-to-day contact with group participants. Leader 2 is assumed to be a former adolescent mother, a community agency staff member, a student intern, or a volunteer.

Session 1   Getting Started

Box 3.1   **Leader Checklist for Session 1**

1. Get-acquainted game sentences are cut out, folded, and in a container ready to use (see page 111).
2. Two or three tables and chairs are set up in a "U" shape in the meeting room.
3. A flip chart or dry erase board is set up with two or three brightly colored markers.
4. Lunch or snack is set out for quick and easy serving.
5. A yellow pad is available to pass around for names and phone numbers.
6. Copies of point system (page 113) and confidentiality handouts (page 112) are ready.

Activities for This Session

This session focuses primarily on helping participants to become acquainted with leaders and other participants, and on helping them to clearly understand the purpose and goals of the group, group norms, and how the group works. This is the beginning stage of the group, and participants will be relying heavily on the leaders to help them be comfortable and open to this experience.

Introductions and Icebreaker

Begin as soon as every participant has settled into eating her lunch or snack. Put the following dialogue into your own words and presentation style, but it should sound something like this:

Leader 1: Welcome. Most of you know that I am _____, your [*school role*].

Leader 2: And I am _____. I was a teen mother, a lot like you. My baby was born when I was ____ years old and in the ____ grade. I will also be leading your group with [*other leader*].

Leader 1: I've met with most of you individually, and you've all agreed to participate in this group. You were invited to join the group because you have already become or will soon become a mother, and because you have great potential for taking charge of your own rapidly changing life! This is pretty early in your life for such a *huge* step as becoming a mother. This is moving you from being a teenager to being a teenager with a child—your baby. Big difference! Some things about becoming a mother can be magical. And some things are such big challenges that they can knock you over if you're not ready for them. This group is about getting ready for the challenges so they don't knock you over, about putting you in charge of your life so that you and your baby can have a life with some good things—some magic in it.

Leader 2: We're going to do some talking and some listening, some learning, and some discovering in here. You will be doing some planning and then taking some action to begin taking charge of the life you want to have. You're going to work on going from "I'm not so sure" to "I know what I want, and I know how to get it."

We're going to start by looking around the room and getting to know one another. So, just look around at everyone. The faces you are looking at right now are all in this with you. They can be a great help to you, and you to them. We hope you will be—and that you will even find friends here who will go on with you when the group is over. It never hurts to have friends who have been where you are and who understand just what you're talking about when you need an ear to listen. _____ [*The co-leader not currently speaking*] is going to pass a "Member ID" sheet around the room right now, and we'd like you to print your name and your phone number on it. We're going to make copies for each of you and give them to you next time, to make it easier for you to remember one another's names and get in touch outside the group.

Some of you may already know one another, and some may not know anybody in here yet. There are people in here you'll get along with better than others, and that's pretty normal. I'm asking you to go one step further. We have 8 [or 12] weeks in here to achieve some important things that can help you out for the rest of your and your children's lives. I'm asking you to be kind and supportive to every girl in this group as much as you can. No matter what it's like outside the group, what the past was, or who your other friends are—in here we are doing important work, and what helps one of us is good for all of us.

Leader 1:   Okay, enough talk from us. We want to hear from you now. Instead of just telling everybody your name, we're going to play a game [Sentence Completion Game, page 111] to help us remember one another better. I'm going to pass this little box around to everyone, and I want you to draw out a slip of paper. On the paper is written the beginning of a sentence. When it is your turn, you will read the part of the sentence that is on your paper, and then complete the sentence as it describes you. For example, here's one for me: "If I could trade places with anyone in the world, it would be _____, because _____."

Well, if I could trade places with anyone in the world, it would be . . . let's see, maybe Oprah, because she's smart and generous, and, oh yes, very rich. [*They'll probably laugh at this. Laugh with them.*] See? That's how it works. So tell us your name and some other thing you'd like us to know about you, and then complete your sentence.

Okay, anyone want to go first? Yes? Then you begin, and we'll go around the room from where you sit. [No? Then we'll start here on my right.] [*Call on each girl in order of seating until everyone, including the other leader, has had a turn introducing herself, completing a sentence, then passing the box to the next person.*]

Group Expectations and Rules

Leader 2:   [*Leader 1 will write on a flip chart sheet as rules are presented.*] There won't be many rules in the group, but we have to have a few ground rules to help us all feel safe and to make everything work. These are the three rules that we have:

1. *Be on time to group.* We only have an hour and 20 minutes to get a lot done every week, so we have to make the most of it! You getting in here and starting on your lunch—that shouldn't be hard!—right at _____ will help us do that.

2. *Come to group every week,* even if you don't feel like it. Every single session is important to you, even if you don't know that yet. It's like any new experience—like doing exercise, maybe. At first it may seem hard, but then you get used to it and look forward to it. *And,* every now and then, everyone at the session will get a little surprise gift when they leave. [*If someone asks, "What kind of little gift?" you might respond, "Well, like movie passes (or whatever you might already know about), maybe. I can't tell you exactly what, because then it wouldn't be a surprise—but you'll like it!"*]

3. *Don't talk about what goes on in the group to outsiders.* Especially don't mention what other members are working on or saying in group to anyone outside the group. If we are going to get our work done in here, we have to feel safe with one another. We can't go around wondering if someone is going to betray us after we share confidential things about ourselves with them. And that rule starts right now. What do you think about that rule? [*Some members will probably have feelings or ideas about this. Listen and*

affirm their comments, maybe saying at some point that trust in one another takes time, and that we have to earn one another's trust.]

We think this rule is so important that we're going to ask you to sign an agreement that you will follow and support this. [*Distribute Confidentiality Agreement found on page 112. Have everyone sign and return.*] Are there other rules that you want to consider? These are our three, but this is your group, and you can also create rules.

Help the group to articulate and discuss their own suggestions, and add them to the first three. Pass out confidentiality agreements for everyone to sign and return to you.

Points System and Awards

Leader 1:   Now that we have the rules out of the way, let's talk about something a lot more fun—awards. In all sincerity, I can tell you that your best, most lasting reward from being in this group will be the skills and ideas that you learn in here. They're going to last you the rest of your life, and you will remember this group for what you learned in here a hundred times before you become an old lady. But because learning new skills and habits is hard work and we all need encouragement when we're learning new and difficult things, there will be an award for you at the end of the group that you can hold in your arms and take home with you—besides your baby! You will work on earning this award simply by doing the things you will be doing whether or not you were going to get an award.

This is how it works. [*Leader 2 distributes the Points System handout found on page 113 and also writes on the flip chart as ways to earn points are discussed. Write the numbers and award titles on the flip chart in bright, readable colors.*]

1.   *You earn 30 points for each group session that you attend.* Already you have earned 30 points for your attendance today. You can earn a possible ____ points by the end of the group just by coming to all the sessions.

2.   *You earn 10 points for each day of school that you attend* from today until the end of the group. You can earn up to ____ points by

attending school every day between today and the end of the group.

3. *You earn 25 points for each task that you complete* toward your personal goals before the group ends in 7 more weeks. Most of you can earn between 200 and 300 points in this way.

4. *You earn 10 points for each extra credit or homework assignment* that you complete. You could earn who knows how many points this way!

At the end of the group, those of you who have earned *at least* _____ points will receive the Outstanding Achievement Award. Those of you who have earned *at least* _____ points will receive the Super Achiever Award.

We will keep up with your attendance and write in your points for group and school attendance on your Points-Earned form every week, which you can see when you come to session. You'll be reporting to us and getting other kinds of confirmation for your task completion points. We'll explain that in the next session.

Ending the Session

You should have 10 to 15 minutes left before the group session ends. During this time, you can summarize the session and invite participants to ask questions about anything from the session that they need clarified or express any concerns they are feeling about the group that they would like to share. Briefly describe the agenda for next week's session.

Summarizing the session should be similar to this:

Leader 2: In this session, we have met one another, and we've talked about some of the things we will be doing and learning in this group. We have talked about the rules that we will follow as members of the group—that we will arrive on time, we will come to all sessions no matter what, and this last one is so important: We will protect the privacy of everyone in here by keeping confidential all the things that are said and done in our group. Finally, we have talked about awards and gifts and how you can earn them. [*Keep this open ended so that participants feel they are permitted to bring up anything they are wondering or worrying about. Keep this discussion to 5 or 6 minutes.*]

Leader 1: What questions or concerns do you have about anything we've done in group today?

Next week we will show you your "points-earned" records and begin adding your points to them every week so you will always know where your points stand.

Leader 2: Next week, I'm going to tell you more about myself. And let me tell you right now—if I can do it, *you* can do it!

Leader 1: Also next week, we will start learning our number one tool, social problem solving—the root of our achievements in the group. Remember that idea: social problem solving. You're going to learn what it is, and how to get started. The time is right now to start learning how to take charge of your own life!

Leader 2: Don't miss the next exciting episode of Taking Charge! [*This is said humorously.*] See you next [day of next session] at [time] right here.

Session 2   The Problem-Solving Process

Box 3.2   **Leader Checklist for Session 2**

---

1. Copies of the problem-solving process handout are ready.

2. A flip chart or dry erase board is set up with two or three brightly colored markers.

3. Three cartoon elephant graphics and one cartoon Cher graphic with sticky backs are ready to use.

4. A lightbulb with double-sided tape on the back is ready to use.

5. Tables and chairs are arranged in a "U."

6. Each member's points have been counted and filled in on her points-earned form.

7. New copies of the weekly points-earned forms are made and ready to give out.

8. Lunch or snack is set up and ready for quick serving.

Activities for This Session

The objective for this session is for group members to gain a beginning understanding of the step-by-step problem-solving process, including choosing goals, barriers to goals, resources and strengths, and strategies for attaining goals. You will use a handout (found on page 114) that diagrams the problem-solving process we use in this group, and continue to write main points on a flip chart as you present them. The coleader will lead the group through an application of the problem-solving process. As you are teaching the group about social problem solving, you should consistently stress your and the group's support for each member as they are learning and beginning to practice these ideas and skills. Emphasize your confidence that each participant is capable of taking charge of her own challenges and goals.

The Social Problem-Solving Process

Leader 1:   First of all, now that we've talked about the social "problem-solving process," we're going to get rid of the word *problem* and use the word *challenge*. [*On the flip chart, strike out the word* problem *and write above it the word* challenge.] A *problem* sounds too much like a giant boulder that has plopped itself down in the middle of your house with the intention of staying forever and making you miserable. A *challenge* is more like an elephant that has lumbered into your living room. [*Tape a cartoon elephant over the word "challenge."*]

You are temporarily dazed by this thing and maybe afraid of it at first. I mean, it looks *big*. But when you think about it, you realize that even though the elephant is a lot bigger than you, and it has the potential to do some real damage, you definitely have some ways to get it out of your living room. See the difference between a rock and an elephant? Between a problem and a challenge? Okay, so instead of problem solving, let's just think of coping with a challenge or removing the elephant from the house.

Okay, so is the first step is to identify your challenges? *No!* Actually, the first step is to identify your *dreams*. [*Distribute the Action Plan for Taking Charge handout found on page 114.*]

What you are looking at here is the same process that is used by big businesses like Intel and Toyota when they want to reach *huge* goals.

Scientists use it when they want to find solutions for diseases like diabetes, for example, or figure out what designs are best to use for running shoes. Believe it or not, a lot of people use these steps to find solutions to their own problems, as well. The most successful people, ones who have achieved amazing things, use this very process. People like Tom Cruise and Cher have answered these same questions, followed this very plan. Did you know that Cher [*attach a cartoon figure or magazine cutout of Cher to flip sheet or board*] had a learning disability called dyslexia? [*Attach the cartoon elephant used before next to Cher.*] That was the elephant in her living room! And did you know that Thomas Edison, the guy who invented light bulbs [*attach lightbulb with two-sided tape to the flip sheet or board*], was hearing impaired and used to get hit with a cane by his teacher at school because she thought he was dumb? [*Attach another elephant next to the lightbulb.*] That was the elephant in his living room. And they both had to find a way to get the big guy out of there—using this kind of process. So we have to figure that what's good for Cher and Thomas Edison is good for us!

Let me just quickly go over the steps in the Action Plan with you, then [*other leader*] is going to get you to help her actually create an example using these steps.

Step 1

Leader 1: Step 1 wants you to answer this question: What dreams do I have for my life? This looks like an easy question, but actually it's a question that takes a lot of thought. Many girls your age have not really thought about what they want for their lives. They think they have a long time—years—before they have to worry about that. Now that you're a mother or going to become a mother, you don't really have that time to not think about these things. Your future has come to meet you early in your life, and this answer will probably take some real consideration.

Step 2

Leader 1: This one requires you to look at the challenges that stand between you and the dreams you have for your life. Why? Because the minute you start identifying the elephants, the barriers, the challenges, whatever you choose to call them, you start moving in on them. They immediately start to lose their power to keep you from getting what you want. But you've got to know what they are before you can start getting them out of your way. So identifying and describing your challenges in a really clear way is *very* important! Otherwise, they slip through your fingers and keep on causing you problems!

Step 3

Leader 1: This question, about treasures, is really about the things you already have going for you. And some of them you probably don't even realize you have. I'm talking about all kinds of things, like maybe that your aunt has volunteered to take care of your baby for you while you're working at Burger King on Saturdays—plus, the fact that you've *got* a job at Burger King on Saturdays! Or that your cousin is always there for you, to listen, or buy you a hamburger, or just to understand. Or . . . well, you tell me. What are some other things you have going for you? Anyone? [*Open for a few contributions, or call on one or two outgoing participants.*] So, in the third step, we're going on this kind of treasure hunt. When you take on an elephant, you may need some help. This is where you find yours!

Step 4

Leader 1: Now in Step 4, you line up the dream, the challenge, and the discoveries you've made of all the things that you already have going for you, and you look at all the possible ways you can think of that you could go about conquering that challenge to get to your dream. You can call these your possible strategies if you want to. Write that out in the margin beside Step 4—"my possible strategies." A strategy is the same thing as a plan, and in Step 4 you're going to write down all the strategies you can think of to get the elephant out of the living room. And the last part of Step 4 is, you have to choose the plan—the strategy—that looks like it will work the best for you.

Step 5

Leader 1: Now that you've chosen the strategy that looks the best to you, you've got to plan for action. What are all the little things that you can do to make sure this plan works? In here, we're going to call these little

things your *tasks*. Write that down in the margin beside Step 5—
"What are my tasks?" [*Leader writes these words down on the flip sheet.*]

I'm talking about little things and big things—but things that you can
do and are going to start doing soon! Want an example? Well, maybe
it's just something like finding a way to get yourself and your baby to
the well-baby clinic for immunizations. Or maybe it's something a
little harder, like talking to your mom or your dad about helping you
out with child care. Things like that—some bigger, some smaller.

Step 6

Leader 1:   This may be the simplest step of all. But it may not be the easiest. This
is where you put your money where your mouth is. Most of the
planning and a lot of the thinking are done by the time you get to this
step. Now it's time for the "A" word—*action!* As they say in the Nike
commercials, we're just going to *do* it. Little bit by little bit, right here
in this group and in between group sessions, you're going to start
moving the elephant out of the house. Step 6 is about giving yourself
a couple of tasks to do every week, and then getting them done! And
then coming back to group and talking to us and your fellow
members about how it went.

And that's it. Those are the six steps of the problem-solving process.
Same ones used by Cher, and a million others!

[*Pause for a few seconds here to change the tone.*]

By now some of you, in your secret heart of hearts, may be ready to
blow me off. You may be saying, "Nah, never happen. Won't work for
me. Too much work. Can't do it." You know . . . all those little things
we tell ourselves when we're facing something new and a little hard.
But I'm asking you to hang on. This is a big job we're asking you to
begin here, but you can do it. And the effort you make is going to pay
off for you over and over for a lot of years. You said you were with us
on this ride, and we're just getting started!

Apply the Steps to Four Goals

The next activity is to lead the group in applying the six steps to an
example. Leader 2 will be leading this one. Before you begin the exercise,

you might spend a couple of minutes telling the group some things that you have accomplished and the difficulties you may have experienced in getting to where you want to be.

Use the flip chart and a marker to write things down where everyone can see as you progress. This is when group members will begin to learn about applying this process to themselves and to see it as possible for them. Even though you will be leading the group through this, it is important that they actively participate. Helping them to participate in this application is your main job in this activity. There is not as much prepared dialogue as you have had up to this point, but the following is a guide for leading the activity.

Leader 2:   To help us focus and stay organized in our goal setting and problem solving in group, we're going to divide our dreams and challenges into four areas. We're going to look at our lives like a pizza, and cut it into four big slices: education, personal relationships, parenting, career. [Draw a circle, divide it into quarters, and then write the four categories in each of the sections as you announce them to the group.]

Shall I explain a little more about what we mean by each one of these? Well, education is pretty easy. It is a dream about school and getting ready for a career. For some of us, the dream may be to finish high school. For some of us, it may be to go to college so we can become a professional of some kind. For some of us, it may be to get technical training so that we can become a dental assistant or a hairstylist. [Tell them about your own training beyond high school.] Whatever is your dream about school or career training and getting ready to take care of yourself in life—that's this one.

Okay, the second one has to do with the relationships in your life. It has to do with your family, your romantic relationships, the people you work with, your boss at work, your teachers, and most especially, the friends you want to have in your life. None of us can live well without people who care about us and support us. This goal is about developing and keeping those relationships plentiful and healthy.

Now, the third one is connected to all the others, because it's about having the skills, the self-confidence, and the support to be a good parent for your child. It's about not only physically caring for your child, but enjoying him, advocating for him, making sure he has what he needs to grow up strong and healthy and happy. Each of you probably has an idea about what you want you goal to be as a parent for your child.

The fourth one, career, has to do with your dreams—where you want to be working, the kind of job you want to be doing, how much money you want to be making, and resources that you'll draw on to help support you and your baby. [*Briefly tell them about choosing your own career.*] As you can see, education and career are very much alike. That's because how much success you have with education leads to how many choices and how much success you'll have with a career.

In summary, what questions do you have about any of these? [*Give members a moment to think before going on.*]

Application Exercise

Leader 2: Okay, now we're going to use our six steps to create our own story about someone similar to you and me, so you can see how this works. And we're going to be working with education, because right now, that's where you can *immediately* make a big difference for yourself.

So, let's describe the girl we're talking about. Now this girl's name should be—what? Anybody have a name for her? [*If someone gives a name, write it down on the flip chart. If not, look around the group and call on someone who has already been verbally participating.*]

Okay, this is _____ we're talking about.

_____ is how old?

Okay, _____ is ____ years old.

What grade is she in? About the _____ grade? At _____ High School [your school].

Okay, now where does she live?

Who lives there with her?

And she's 5 months pregnant.

Who is the baby's father?

Does he also go to school?

How old is he?

What is their relationship like? [*Continue writing all these points on the chart.*]

Okay, let's review here. We're telling a story about _____, who is _____ years old. _____ is in the _____ grade at _____ high school. She lives with _____, and she is 5 months pregnant. The father of her baby is _____, and he _____ [also goes to school, works, is unemployed, etc.]. He's _____ years old. Currently, their relationship is _____.

Now, with her baby due in 4 more months, _____ realizes that her life is going to change drastically pretty soon, and she wants to be as prepared for that as she can be. She's thinking that if she doesn't take charge of things, she may have to give up some dreams that are very important to her.

So, looking at this action plan, what is _____'s goal for her education? Is it to pass all her classes this semester? Is it to pass to the next grade next year? Is it to graduate this year? Is it to improve her math grade or her science grade? [*Turn to the group, inviting discussion and suggestions. Write them down on the flip chart.*]

Okay, we have some great goals here. Which one do we want to follow? [*Take a vote.*]

Okay, we have an important education goal that _____ wants to achieve for herself. Now to Step 2: Does _____ have any elephants standing between her and achieving her goal? Most likely she does have a few elephants to get out of the way. What are these challenges? What would be an elephant for *you*? [*Look to members for comments and ideas. If no one responds, call on someone. If the group is unable to provide ideas at this point, you can suggest a challenge, such as "being able to attend school enough days to pass my work."]*

Let's look a little closer at this. What would be some reasons why attending school every day would be a problem for _____?
[The group may say things like "the baby being sick," "medical appointments," or "problems with child care." If not, you can suggest some of these and ask their opinions about the legitimacy of these reasons. Write them on the flip chart under School Attendance. Repeat the process for other suggested challenges to education and career training.]

[Moving to Step 3, use a new sheet on the flip chart. Distinguish the challenges with a word or two, and number them when you begin identifying resources under each.]

Now for Step 3. This is like a treasure hunt, because what we're going to uncover here really are little treasures that _____ can use to help her knock out these little and big challenges. Let's look again at the challenges, because we're looking for the resources that will help with them specifically, even though these little treasures may help with other challenges as they come up, also. So, look at the first challenge under education and career training. What little treasures does _____ already have going for her? These can be treasures from her family, her friends, her neighborhood, or school, or even personal qualities that she has. Let's look at her resources for dealing with the challenge of _____.

Take the group through as many resources as they can identify. Examples that you could suggest to help them out are these:

- Cousins who like to take care of her baby sometimes

- A friend who doesn't mind driving her to appointments sometimes

- Her own "stubbornness." (She could insist on after-school appointments with her food stamp worker or the well-baby clinic.)

- School options in her district other than regular day school

- Her supportive mother, even though she works and usually cannot provide child care

- Two brothers, two aunts, and an uncle who help out when possible

- Her past work experience at a fast-food restaurant

Leader 2:   Now we're ready for Step 4. We're planning for action. Looking at the challenges that _____ is facing in her education goal, and then at the resources that she has, let's decide, what are some possible strategies that she could use to conquer this challenge to her dream for school and education?

List all that are suggested, offering a couple or calling on specific participants if no one volunteers. For example, if the challenge is "missing too much school because her aunt, who currently takes care of the baby during school hours for free, is unavailable 1 or more days every week," some possible strategies could be these:

- Getting more friends and family involved in providing child care

- Getting a job to pay for a child-care center

- Going to night school instead of during the day, so her own mother can babysit

- Developing a backup plan for child care when her aunt is unavailable

Leader 2:   Okay, here we have four possible strategies for overcoming this challenge. Which one of these has the best chance of working? Let's talk about each of them.

Take each strategy in turn, and invite the group to discuss its pros and cons. You will probably arrive at a consensus in this way. If not, take a vote.

Leader 2:   Now for Step 5. What steps can she take? What little jobs can she do in order to carry out the strategy that we have just picked?

Use a new sheet in the flip chart. Once again, describe the challenge and the resolution strategy briefly, and underneath write tasks as the group suggests them. For example, if the strategy selected is to develop a backup plan for when her aunt is unavailable, some immediate tasks might be these:

- Ask another relative or friend if they would be willing to provide child care when her aunt is unavailable.

- Call the state daycare referral office to inquire about drop-in or part-time day-care facilities that could provide care when her aunt was unavailable.

- Visit one or more day-care providers to learn about costs and conditions for drop-in or part-time care for when her aunt is not available.

Leader 2:   Okay, let's review what we've done. [*Begin with the identifying information about the girl, and briefly go through the steps and the points you and the group have made at each step.*] We have gone through the entire planning process. The only step left is the doing! That is the step *you* will be doing both in and out of group starting next week. For right now, though, let me say that you guys have done great work today. You caught on quickly, you had brilliant ideas, and you stuck with it until we finished. I feel very encouraged about the things you're going to accomplish over the next few weeks. Next week, you'll be starting on your own action plan.

Ending the Session

You will probably have only a few minutes left until the end of the session. Pass out written reports to each member showing the number of points she has earned so far, and the source of the points.

Leader 1:   We have only a couple of minutes left. What questions or concerns do you have about today's session? Okay, then, next week we'll be ready to go for it with our own goals!

Box 3.3   **Leader Checklist for Session 3**

---

1. Tables and chairs are arranged in a "U."

2. A flip chart or dry erase board is set up with two or three brightly colored markers.

3. Lunch or snack is set up and ready for quick serving.

4. Each member's points have been counted, added to her points-earned form, and placed in her folder.

5. Four copies for each member of the problem-solving worksheet have been made.

6. Eight copies for each member of the task work sheets have been made.

7. Four problem-solving worksheets and eight task worksheets have been placed in a pocketed folder for each member.

8. There are enough sharpened pencils with good erasers to provide for each member.

9. Little gifts for those present are in a container ready to be given at end of session.

Activities of This Session

Every member should work through the first five steps of the problem-solving process in the area of education. This should include identifying goal, challenges, underlying challenges, resources, possible solution strategies, picking a strategy, and planning tasks. By the end of this session, each member should have completed this process for a goal in education.

Three Segments of This Session

1.   Review the basic problem-solving steps while members have lunch or snack. This should take 20 to 25 minutes. You will need extra time for the second segment, so you may want to shorten this initial segment if possible.

2. Remain as a whole group or break into subgroups that you will have designated, and members will discuss education goals and begin working the problem-solving process on education. They will use a goal worksheet that you give them, found on page 115.

3. Briefly review the session, including reading to the group and affirming a couple of the tasks that have been selected for the coming week. Invite questions and concerns. Identify personal relationships as the goal for the next session.

At this session, each participant who attended should receive a small gift as she leaves the session.

Review Basics of Problem-Solving Process

Leader 1: Everybody, today you start taking charge! I'm pretty sure that all kinds of things during the week have pushed most of what we did last week to the back of your mind. So while you're having your lunch, I want to review a little from what we did last week, just to refresh us. [*Use the flip chart sheet that you used to identify the steps from last session to go over the steps.*]

Leader 2: Remember _____, the hero of our story last week? [*Refer to flip chart sheets used in the last session.*] I want us quickly to go over that story. As I'm going over this, if you have had more ideas about it since last week, just jump in with them when I come to that part. One important thing to remember is that we can always change what we first plan if that seems logical after we think more about it or learn something that makes us want to change any part of a strategy.

Using last session's flip chart sheets as a visual reference, briefly go through the applied process from last week. When you have completed that, you are ready to break the group into two smaller groups or remain in the larger group to work on education goals and tasks.

Discuss and Work on Education Goal

Leader 1: Now we're going to split ourselves into two smaller groups to start our work. We'll be doing this for part of each session from here on out. This doesn't mean that you can't talk to members or the leader in the other group. You can still get their advice or consult with them any time. It is just easier to give you more attention and help when we're working in a smaller group. So, [name members of one small group] will form a smaller group over here [designate area of room] with [Leader 2] as their leader. And these members [name members of second small group] will be the other small group over here [designate area] with me as their leader. Move to your designated areas, and arrange a table so that your group can sit around it to work together and help one another.

You will need to walk among members around the table much of the time during this working segment.

Leaders 1 and 2 [in respective small groups]: First, let me distribute your work folders and pencils. Each folder contains four goal worksheets, eight task planners, and eight task-verification forms. [*Distribute pencils and folders with forms (pages 115, 116, and 118).*]

Today we're going to work on a goal for education, just as we worked out for our hero _____. So take out just one of the goal worksheets, and let's begin. [*Have the group fill in their name and "Education" in the designated areas at the top.*]

Spend a few minutes thinking about your dream in this area. This is about you being successful in high school or maybe education beyond high school, like a community college degree or a training school certification. Think about someone you know—maybe a little older than you—who is doing well at school, or who has even gone on to college. Think about what *you* would like to achieve in school. It could be passing all your subjects this semester, or it could be to pass the grade you're in this year, or it could be to pass history or science. What do you see when you imagine yourself making your best achievement with school? [*Encourage verbal responses. Call on one or two of the group if no one volunteers. Go around the table as you are talking, and look at what some of the members are writing for their goal. Give a thumbs up, a smile, a look of pleased surprise—anything that affirms their work. If an occasional member does not want you to acknowledge or interact with her at this point in her process, simply focus on others.*]

Would you like to talk a minute about the goal you've written down? You've got some great ones from what I just saw on your worksheets, and I think you could help one another out if we share them. [*Take a few minutes to hear and affirm goals from the group. It is okay if not everyone volunteers to talk.*]

Now let's move on to the biggest challenge that stands between you and this goal. Think about it for a minute, and let's hear them before you write them down. [*At this point, they may also begin to have some questions, or need clarification. Encourage each member to share her ideas about her biggest challenge in this area, and invite suggestions and feedback when possible.*]

Now keep thinking about this big elephant here, and write down all the little things that make it such a challenge. Don't throw in things just to be negative. Stick to the real obstacles that we have to work on here. [*Ask members to share the underlying obstacles they have identified.*]

Okay, now this is kind of the fun part. But it can be hard, too, if you're not used to thinking about all the good things about yourself and your life. I want you to just start writing a list of all the people in your life who help you out a lot, along with how they help you out. Then I want you to write down all the situations in your life that help you out—maybe that you have a part-time job, or you have a car, or you live only a block from school—anything like that. Then I want you—and this may be the hardest for some of you—to write down things about yourself that come in handy when you're trying to get something done. Things that you are proud of or that people have told you about yourself, that you can consider little treasures and qualities that you have going for you. What are some that we came up with when we were doing the exercise about _____, our hero girl? [*Have the group recall some of the resources they gave during that exercise.*]

Now I know that most of you have at least one or two of those resources of your own. Use those to start your list. Okay—go! [*Spend some time going around the group sharing about these resources. It is important that participants take these in as their real strengths and assets.*]

I want you to remember where in your folder you put this list of strengths and assets, because every now and then I'm going to ask you to add to it. Keep that in mind at all times! [*Smile. (And remember to do this!)*]

Okay, let's move on to the next step, which is to brainstorm. You know what brainstorming is? [*Some members probably know this concept. Ask them to explain it to the group. Then you add more explanation and relate it to this step.*]

Now I want you to brainstorm all the possible strategies that you can use to achieve this goal. Just write down everything that you can think of, and use this list of strengths and assets as you're coming up with these strategies. [*If members have a hard time getting started, take a few minutes and use one member's process to brainstorm some possible strategies with the group. Then give them a few minutes to come up with their own.*]

Now I want you to look at each one of the possible strategies you've got there, and think to yourself about how things would likely turn out if you tried that one. Would it work? What are the reasons it would work? What are some things that might keep it from working? And when you have done that with each one, choose the one that you think will work the best. Write it down on your worksheet. [*Ask who would like to share with the group the strategy they've chosen. If everyone is hesitant, ask a particular member who has a strategy that others could benefit from hearing.*]

Now we're almost there. The last thing you need to do is look at this strategy, and figure out what you need to do to get it done. Figure out two tasks—no more than that—that you can do *this week* to carry out this strategy. These need to be things in addition to coming to school every day, because you're already doing that to earn your points. So, two additional tasks. You may add some other tasks as you go along, after you've gotten these first ones taken care of, but for right now, just concentrate on two things you can do this week—before our next session—to get your strategy done. Think about this for a couple of minutes—think about when you will do each task, any help you may need, including encouragement, babysitting, or anything else that you need to think of. Then write them down on your task planner [*hold up task planner form*]. And fill in the details like when, where, how you're going to do it. [*Ask each member to identify one of her tasks to share with the group, and talk about these for a few minutes. Praise the group for all the work they have done in this session. At this beginning point the members need support and encouragement more than later when the process is more familiar and they are feeling more competent with it.*]

Be sure to take your task verification forms with you today. You'll need to have someone sign one for each task, who was with you or helped you do the task. Bring them back next week.

If you are ready to earn extra points for your homework or extra credit assignments, we have forms for your teacher to sign [found on page 120] and for you to bring back next week.

Ending the Session

Bring small groups back together for reviewing the session and preparing for the next session. Be at the door when they begin to leave, so that you can present their gifts—tell them it is for all their hard work. Also give each member her session points tally (see page 123). Be generous with the praise and compliments today! And praise yourselves as well. This is a difficult session.

Session 4   The Relationships Goal

Box 3.4   Leader Checklist for Session 4

---

1. Tables and chairs are arranged in a "U."

2. A flip chart or dry erase board is set up with two or three brightly colored markers.

3. Points have been tallied, weekly points-earned forms completed and placed in participant folders.

4. Participant folders are ready for distribution.

5. Lunch or snack is set up and ready for quick serving.

Activities for This Session

First, participants should evaluate their task performance from the previous week and plan further work on their education goal, such as performing tasks not attempted, strategizing new approaches for tasks attempted but not completed, or adding a new task.

Second, each participant should work the problem-solving process for a personal relationships goal. By the end of the session, each member should have two tasks to perform for this goal during the week.

Review Tasks of the Past Week

During the first 25 minutes of the session while participants are having lunch, you have two topics to discuss with the group. Leader 1, take about 10 minutes to review group members' experiences with their tasks during the previous week. Encourage participants to share experiences in performing their tasks, and help them if they are hesitant or vague.

Be empathetic, and also joke a little to lighten the moment when possible. Above all, be supportive, give a lot of praise, and frame their setbacks as normal and conquerable. The following are some examples of supportive responses about problems with the tasks:

- Great work! It's perfectly normal for you to feel that way—this is your first try at something like this.

- I know this is hard for you to believe, but you've picked a challenging task here, and you're doing great so far.

- You've just got to peel this one like layers on an onion, don't you? I can't believe you got that far. One more go at it ought to do the trick.

- Hey, you're way ahead of most people your age on this one. I cannot tell you how much that impresses me.

  Leader 1 will take the lead in this discussion, although leader 2 should also make comments and participate as well.

Discuss and Work on Personal Relationships Goal

Now switch, and engage the group in a discussion about personal relationships. This should be instructive as well as involve group members. Leader 2, open the flip chart to a clean page, and pick up a marker.

Leader 2: Okay, now we're going to talk about something that's going to be awful for you to even think about—the thing every woman hates to talk about most: [*pause a moment*]—men. [*This is a joke, so be funny with it. They will laugh with you. Then pause again.*] Well, actually, we're going to talk about all kinds of personal relationships—but men are a big part of that topic.

Leader 2: What I want us to do right now is make a list on the flip chart of the personal relationships we consider most important in our lives. I am going to write them down as you call them out. Okay, tell us!

[*Leader 1, try to call on one at a time, but if they get really involved, just try to write down all that you can. They will probably name boyfriends and mothers first, then fathers, siblings, friends, and other family members.*]

Leader 2: Okay, now that we have our list, I want us to put a star beside the relationships that we have the most trouble with. It can be several of these. Okay, tell us. [*Repeat the above process, putting an asterisk beside the relationships they call out.*]

Leader 1: Let's take a look at the troublesome relationships we've identified here. For example, some of you have said that one of the relationships you have the most trouble with is your relationship with the man in your life, whether he's your husband, your boyfriend, or the father of your baby. What are some of the problems in this relationship? [*Draw a vertical line down the middle of a new flip sheet; write problems on the left side of the line.*]

Okay, how would you like for this relationship to be? What would you like to be different? [*Write these down on the right side of the line.*]

That gives us a pretty good look at relationships with the men in your lives. Let's look at another relationship—you've said that your relationship with your mother is also one where you have problems. What are the problems in this relationship? [*Draw a line down the middle of a new sheet, and write problems on the left side.*]

How would you like for this relationship to be? If it were just the way you want it to be, what would be different? [*Write these things down on the right side.*]

Okay, from working on these two, nearly everyone has a head start on their personal relationships goal. Get into your groups with all these things in your mind that we have just talked about, and get going on your worksheets—most of you have already done some of your thinking on this!

In your small groups, take participants through the problem-solving steps much the same way that you did last session. Ask if anyone has other relationships that they want to focus on other than the two that the group processed. Be available to work more closely with these in helping to identify problems and goals.

When you have 12 to 15 minutes left in small group time, ask participants to identify work that still needs to be done on last week's tasks. Some will have completed their tasks from last week. Others will have accomplished some or very little of their tasks. With them, it is time to offer help. Call on one or two participants who did not get tasks completed and ask questions like these to help develop a new strategy for getting the task done:

- What kept you from getting the task done?

- What can happen differently this week to get this one out of the way?

- Who do you want to help you with it? Remember, help can be as simple as talking about it before you do it—or as involved as going with you to do it—or anything in between. We are here to help. Pick one of us to help you.

- Okay, now what do you need [person she named] to do?

- When will you get together with [same person just named] to get help?

Encourage the participant to choose another group member or yourself to help her, although it is okay if she prefers a specific person outside the group. Help each member who has unfinished tasks to be as specific as possible about when, where, and how she will get the task done.

Ending the Session

Bring the small groups together to summarize this session and prepare for the next session. If there is not time, do the following with each of your small groups: (1) Give participants their cumulative and session points (pages 121 and 122) that you tallied before the session, (2) remind them that points earned for attendance and tasks today will be added to next week's total, and (3) be supportive and encourage their task work on personal relationships. Relationship work is emotionally risky and is the area where adolescents tend to have the shortest range of personal resources to deal with distress.

Session 5   The Parenting Goal

Box 3.5   **Leader Checklist for Session 5**

---

1. Tables and chairs are arranged in a "U."

2. A flip chart or dry erase board is set up with two or three brightly colored markers.

3. Participant points have been counted, filled in on points-earned forms, and placed in participant folders.

4. Lunch or snack is set up and ready for quick serving.

Activities for This Session

The goal for Session 5 is on parenting. The first group activity in the session is for members to process their task experiences with personal relationships from the previous week and make plans for those tasks not yet accomplished. The second activity is for members to work the problem-solving process, identifying a parenting goal and two tasks to work on during the coming week.

Review Tasks of the Past Week

Session 5's structure is similar to Session 4's. The first 25 minutes of the session follow the same format that you followed in Session 4. Discuss participants' experiences with their relationship tasks during the previous week. Expect a great deal of group response in this discussion. You are now in the 5th week, and members are feeling more trusting and comfortable sharing their experiences and feelings with the group about almost any topic. Also, this is a highly charged topic for an adolescent group, and some members may have put more effort into these tasks than with previous goals. Expect them to have a number of stories to tell. Keep up your empathetic responses, but be open to a little joking and humor as well. This discussion can provide support and reassurance to your participants as well as be a strong bonding experience for the group. Refer to Session 4, and use the same types of questions and supportive responses in this discussion that you used in that session.

Discuss and Work on Parenting Goal

Your second objective during the initial 25 minutes is to engage the group in thinking about their challenges in the area of parenting. Structure this discussion by following primarily the same split-page process that you used in helping the group to identify relationship issues last week. Draw a vertical line on the flip chart sheet, and ask members to identify *problems* with parenting on the left, and what the *solution* would look like on the right.

For the small group period of identifying goals and tasks related to parenting, refer to Sessions 3 and 4. Follow a similar process for helping members to develop goals, strategies, and tasks that you followed in these sessions.

During the last 15 or so minutes of the small group session, participants should again evaluate their task performance from the previous week. There may not be time to work on undone tasks prior to last week, unless a member specifically asks for help with a previous task. Otherwise, these will be saved for Session 7. Ask the group how members managed with their "catch-up" tasks during the week. Here in the 5th session, expect other participants to actively engage in this discussion. In fact, it is good if the group more or less takes over its own discussion and you can take a quieter, less directive role.

Here are some questions you might use to guide you:

- So, who knocked off an old task during this past week?

- Will you tell us how it went?

- What did you do differently than before?

- How did you use [person they identified to help them] to help?

- Who needs help during the coming week with a task from last week that they didn't get done?

Follow the procedure you used in Session 4 for setting up new strategies and getting helpers for those who need them.

Ending the Session

In the 15-minute summary, give each participant her current points record that you have tallied before the session. Continue to give a lot of praise and encouragement for the work they are doing! Even though they are well into the group by now, they still see you as an authority that legitimates and affirms what they are doing, and they still need your positive responses. Ask about their questions or last-minute comments. Remind them that next week's goal area will be employment and careers.

Session 6   The Career Goal

Box 3.6   **Leader Checklist for Session 6**

---

1. Tables and chairs are arranged in a "U."

2. A flip chart or dry erase board is set up with two or three brightly colored markers.

3. Lunch or snack is set up and ready for quick serving.

4. Little gifts in bags or envelopes ready to present at end of session.

5. Points for each member have been tallied, recorded in weekly points-earned forms, and placed in participant folders.

6. Extra task confirmation forms are available.

Activities for This Session

The topic for Session 6 is employment and careers. By this session, you and the group have developed a sense of familiarity and comfort with the group processes and activities, as well as with your respective roles. You know what to expect from one another most of the time, and hopefully, the group has begun to take responsibility for much of its own work.

The group's primary activities for this session are these: (1) Each participant should work the problem-solving process to identify her goal, problems, strategies, and two tasks related to employment or a desired career; and (2) to process her tasks with the group and make plans to complete tasks that she did not complete last week.

Review Tasks of the Past Week

Session 6's structure is similar to that of Sessions 4 and 5. The first 25 minutes of the session should be devoted to discussing participants' experiences with their parenting tasks during the previous week. Because you are now in the 6th week, you should expect members to freely share their experiences, feelings, and mistakes with the group. Also, parenting for young mothers is closely woven into their personal relationships, so be prepared for some crossover and continued discussion of relationship with baby's father or their own mothers. Again, expect them to have a number of stories to tell. Refer to the list of suggested questions and comments in Session 4, and draw on these in this discussion.

Discuss and Work on Employment and Career Goal

Employment and career is an important goal area and one that requires special attention to the range of ages and grades represented in the group. Although it is an immediate goal for older participants, younger members who still have 2 or more years of school may not be ready to act on it. Consequently, there may be a wide range of goals and tasks in this area. It is appropriate for younger participants to form tasks primarily to inform them for further planning, whereas older participants may create tasks that actually put them into the job market or career training. For example, although both a 15-year-old and an 18-year-old may have the career goal of becoming a legal assistant, the 15-year-old may select the task of finding out where she can get the training, how long it takes, and what financial aid is available. The 18-year-old may choose a more immediate task such as making an appointment with a counselor to begin enrolling in the training program. This is a point of difference that you need to emphasize when you lead the group through identifying employment and career issues while they are having lunch.

Use the following questions to guide the group through this discussion. It may help the group to focus if you write everything on the flip chart.

Leader 2: Okay, let's just start with another list. We're getting good at these lists. Let's just make a list of our dreams. Now, most of us are in our jobs *a lot* of hours every week, and you will be, too. Therefore, we want them to be jobs that we enjoy—that we're interested in—don't we? What do you want to do in your career? What do you want your job to be? [*Write them down the middle of the flip sheet with a marker as they are called out.*]

Okay! What a list! These are *wonderful* career dreams! Tell me, what are some extra advantages—besides liking what you do for a living—when you get into one of these? [*Go for responses such as "good money," "respect," "steady work," or "lots of jobs available." Use a different color marker and write these responses down on the same flip chart sheet in the margins and all around where you have written the list.*]

Leader 1: All right, tell me the challenges that you're going to have to face on the way to getting into these wonderful careers. [*Write these down the middle of a new flip chart sheet.*]

Okay, one more—what are some strategies you can use *right now* that can make these challenges smaller? [*Write these with a different color, in the margins and all around the list. You are looking for responses such as good grades in school, graduating, learning about training programs and financial aid, taking courses in high school that prepare for careers.*]

Separate into small groups to continue the process. Tape the flip chart sheets you used in your discussion on the wall so they are visible to everyone. Follow the same process of developing goals and tasks that you followed in previous sessions.

Ending the Session

During your summary at the end of today's session

1. Ask the group to think this week of the tasks that they still need to get done, because next session will be about bringing them all up to date.

2. Give them the points-earned tallies that you have prepared.

3. Present each one with a small gift as they leave.

4. Give abundant words of recognition, encouragement, and support!

Session 7   Catching Up

Box 3.7   **Leader Checklist for Session 7**

1. Tables and chairs are arranged in a "U."

2. Lunch or snack is set up and ready for quick serving.

3. A flip chart or dry erase board is set up with two or three brightly colored markers.

4. Extra copies of goal and task worksheets and task confirmations are available.

5. Points for each participant have been tallied, recorded in weekly points-earned forms and placed in participant folders.

Activities for This Session

Today's session will be similar in format to the previous 4 sessions, although participants will focus on catching up with past tasks rather than taking on new ones. You will also begin the process of ending the group. Your two primary activities for the session are these:

1. Members will process experiences with tasks during the past week, as well as previous tasks that they may not have completed, and plan how they will complete, change, or drop unfinished tasks.

2. The group will talk about ending after 1 more session and begin to identify what that means to the members.

Review Tasks of the Past Week

In the initial 25-minute period, first engage the group in processing their past-week task experiences, following the same procedures that you have used in the past 4 sessions.

Begin Discussing Termination

When you have about 10 minutes left in this period, change the discussion to the group ending after 1 more session. If you feel comfortable doing so, leaders may jointly facilitate this discussion. It should go something like this:

Leader 1 or 2: You women know, we have only 1 more session after today. This means that today we need to each take a good look at the work we still have to do this week—catch up on points if we're behind—and just start thinking about what it will be like not to have our group anymore. Are there going to be good things about not having group every week? [*This is more in the vein of beginning to think of termination rather than actual processing, so you need not write it down. Expect members to joke about termination at this point, as a way of dealing with their feelings. They may jokingly talk about how bad the food has been, or how hard they've had to work, or having to put up with one another. Laugh with them about these, but realize also that they are probably experiencing some feelings that are uncomfortable and maybe scary.*]

I think it is hard to say good-bye to the group, even though most of us will still see one another here at school. It won't be the same as having this time together in group.

We are wondering if you would like to plan something special for our last session. Would you like to have a celebration cake or some other special treat? What do you think? [*If they have other suggestions, write them on a flip chart sheet, discuss the pros and cons, and take a vote.*]

Work on Task Catch-Up

Break into small groups.

1. Go through every participant's goals and tasks, completed or not.

2. Have each participant choose two tasks that she has not yet accomplished and strategize how she can get them done during this week, using essentially the same procedures that you used in Sessions 3 through 6.

3. Have members designate someone to help them with the remaining tasks.

Ending the Session

Bring small groups back together about 15 minutes before the end of the session. Tell the group that next week they will take a break at the end of the session, then return to the room to receive their final awards. If possible, you will need to arrange with the school for each participant to miss her first afternoon class period on that day. Make sure everyone in the group is clear about these arrangements—answer all their questions fully and clearly. Give each participant her points tally for this session.

Session 8   Ending the Group

Box 3.8   **Leader Checklist for Session 8**

1. Tables and chairs are arranged in a "U."

2. Lunch or snack is set up and ready for quick serving.

3. Cake (or other treat) with a celebration message is ready to be served.

4. A flip chart or dry erase board is set up with two or three brightly colored markers.

5. Final award items are waiting in leader's office to be presented to members.

6. Certificates of completion for each member have been signed by both leaders.

7. Points earned by each participant have been tallied, recorded in weekly points-earned forms, and placed in participant folders.

Activities for This Session

The primary objective for this session is for participants to terminate the group with an awareness of what they have accomplished and how they can use these changes and skills in their lives. Although you will work in small groups for a few minutes in this session, most of the time will be spent in the large group.

Review Accomplishments

Leader 1:   Well, here we are in our last session. I think we need to do some bragging about the things we've accomplished these past 2 months. I'm wondering what some of you are thinking about, as you get ready to leave the group. Anybody want to say?

■   Okay, who wants to tell us about their biggest accomplishment?

■   Think of all the tasks you've done during these weeks—which one was the hardest to do?

■   Which made a big difference in your life? Think of that special one, and tell us about it.

[Write responses on a flip sheet with a marker. You will probably get responses to this invitation, but if not quickly enough for the limited time, call on a participant whom you know has carried out a particularly difficult or meaningful task and ask her to share it.]

■   Now another question: What has been the hardest thing you have had to do in the group? Come on—I know you've all struggled and worked really hard. I'm so proud of you! What was the hardest part of it? *[Affirm the responses and write them on a flip sheet.]*

■   Okay, one more question, and this one is for every one of us: What is one thing you have learned about yourself or something in your life from being in the group? I'll start, and then let's go around this way *[right or left]* and everyone take a turn, and we'll end with *[other leader]*.

What you share with the group that you have learned about yourself should come genuinely out of your experience with the group. It can be a strength that you did not realize you had and are now appreciating, or even traits that you do not especially like, never noticed, and want to work on changing.

When you finish this exercise, conclude this part of the session with something like this:

Leader 2:   It sounds like most of us have been changed by the group in some way, that we have learned things and gained skills we didn't have before. It is important for us to realize this. Now listen: Just because the group is ending does not mean that you lose the things you have gained in here. These are skills, knowledge, ideas, and goals that you take with you from now on. That's what this entire thing was about. Hang onto them! When you are with one another, or even when you're alone, remind yourself of what you know and what you can do! Don't ever forget that an elephant is just an elephant—and you can move an elephant.

Discuss and Review Final Tasks

1. Members finish paperwork for tasks they have accomplished during the past week.

2. Members recount to the small group all the tasks they have accomplished over the duration of the group.

3. Members add the points they have gained since last session to their current total and calculate a preliminary points total before they leave the group today.

Ending the Session

When you have finished the above three activities, bring the groups back together and cut the celebration cake or serve the other special treats. While members are eating and talking among themselves, you can tally final points (form on page 121) for each member to determine awards. When you have done this, you might lead the group in an ending ritual something like this:

1. Ask each member to come forward when her name is called, and present her with a certificate of completion signed by both leaders. As each participant is called, announce the award and present it with her certificate.

2. As each member comes forward, make a sincere, affirming comment about your observations of her during the group. For example, "Sonia Perez has been a friend to everyone in here. She has helped several of you with your tasks, and she always has a good word. She is the kind of friend we all want to have."

3. In conclusion, each leader should make an affirming comment about your impressions of the group or your experience in leading the group.

Extending the Taking Charge Group

Young mothers have often expressed a desire to continue with the group after 8 sessions. These are some responses members have given in support of extending the group:

- It gave them something to look forward to every week at school.
- It helped them to focus on what they needed to be doing.
- It gave them a social time with others in their situation.
- It was a place where they felt heard and understood.
- It gave them a sense of confidence when they confronted difficult situations.

Although the original Taking Charge curriculum and treatment manual includes only 8 sessions, some schools using the group have extended it to 12 sessions, lasting until the end of the semester in which it was presented. Most groups opt to use extra weeks for extending each goal area to 2 sessions. Overall, they report that giving participants 2 weeks for each goal in which to complete tasks appears to result in accomplishing more tasks and in attempting more difficult and emotional risk-taking behaviors and skills.

Summary

This chapter contains step-by-step guidance instructing leaders on how to facilitate each session of the Taking Charge group curriculum. Forms and material needed to facilitate each session were also provided. This chapter serves as a training manual and includes detailed instructions and dialogue for leaders to follow when conducting the groups to assure the best intervention fidelity. This manual is practice oriented and intended to serve as a leader's guide for each group session. To use this chapter as a training tool, it should be presented in a training group, where it can best provide practice and clarification opportunities for the new leaders. It is not recommended, however, that this chapter be used in leadership training groups until potential leaders have read the entire contents of this book.

Forms and Handouts

On the following pages are forms for group leaders and handouts for group participants. They are copy-ready and in the order in which they are to be used in leading the Taking Charge group.

Introduction Game for Session 1

Cut out these statements separately, fold each, and put into a container. Each member draws one as the container is passed and it is her turn to introduce herself. After telling her name and something about herself, she reads her statement, completing it as it applies to her.

My favorite time of day is _____ because _____.

If I could live anywhere in the world, I would live _____ because _____.

When I was a little girl, my favorite food was _____. Now it is _____.

The person I enjoy talking to most is _____ because _____.

When I was little, my favorite toy was _____. Now my favorite "toy" is _____.

If I could have any job in the world, I would like to be _____, because _____.

My idea of a perfect day is when I can _____.

The person I most want to be like is _____ because _____.

My favorite holiday is _____ because then I usually _____.

My favorite TV show is _____ because _____.

If I could have any pet, I would want a _____ because _____.

A perfect vacation for me would be _____.

I like to get presents from _____ because _____.

My favorite relative is _____ because _____.

The thing I like best about my baby's father is _____.

The thing I like least about my baby's father is _____.

Something I've always wanted to do but haven't gotten to yet is _____.

Confidentiality Agreement

As a member of the Taking Charge group at my school, I, _____, agree to keep confidential everything that I learn about my fellow group members in our group sessions. This means that I agree to not talk about anyone in my group with anyone outside the group, even with my family, my friends, or my boyfriend/husband.

_____   _____
Signature   Date

Taking Charge

Great Rewards Point System

Each day that I attend *school* = 10 points

Each session that I attend *group* = 25 points

Each *task* I perform for myself = 25 points

Each *homework* assignment I do = 10 points

Each *extra credit* assignment I do = 10 points

I will receive the *achievement award* if I earn at least 450 points.

I will receive the *outstanding achievement award* if I earn at least 600 points.

Action Plan for Taking Charge

Step 1   Answer this question: What do I want to be *different* in my life?

Step 2   Answer this question: What *barrier* stands between me and the thing I want to be different?

Step 3   Answer this question: What *treasures* do I have in myself and in my life that can help me to get past these barriers?

Step 4   Answer these questions: What are some possible *strategies* that I can follow to get past the barriers? Which strategy is likely to work best?

Step 5   Answer this question: What are *two things I can do immediately* to carry out my strategy?

Step 6   Now, as the Nike commercial says, *just do it!!*

Goal Worksheet

_____   _____
Name   Goal area

Step 1 My goal is _____

Step 2 The biggest barrier to reaching my goal is _____

_____ .

Smaller things that make this barrier a big problem are

1. _____

2. _____

3. _____

Step 3 I have resources to help me. The best ones are

1. _____   4. _____

2. _____   5. _____

3. _____   6. _____

Step 4 These are possible strategies I can follow to defeat my problem:

1. _____

2. _____

3. _____

Number _____ seems the most likely plan to succeed. I'm going to try it.

Step 5 Two things (tasks) that I can do immediately to start reaching my goal are

1. _____

2. _____

Task Planner

First Task for

_____   _____
Group member   Goal area

Strategy:_____

Description of task: _____

_____

What I will do to accomplish this task: _____

I will do this by _____, and I will ask _____ for help if I need it.

_____   _____
Date   Helper

Second Task for _____

_____   _____
Group member   Goal area

Strategy: _____

Description of task: _____

_____

What I will do to accomplish this task: _____

I will do this by _____ and ask _____ for help if I need it.

_____   _____
Date   Helper

_____   _____
Signature   Date

What Happened to My First Task

I (did) _____ (did not) _____ get this task done this week. This is what happened:

My evidence that I completed this task is:

This is what I plan to do next:

What Happened to My Second Task

I (did) _____ (did not) _____ get this task done this week. This is what happened:

My evidence that I completed this task is:

This is what I plan to do next:

_____   _____
Signature   Date

Task Verification for the Taking Charge Group

_____ School

Dear Contact:

The person presenting this form to you, _____, needs
verification that she has done the task described below. As her contact in carrying out this task, please
verify by signing your name and your phone number. We would like to be able to contact you, if
necessary. Thank you for your help.

Sincerely,

Group Leader

Task performed:

_____   _____   _____
Signature of Contact   Telephone   Date

Homework and Extra Credit Verification

This is to verify that _____ completed

_____ homework or _____ extra credit assignment on

_____   _____   _____
Date   Teacher   Course

Homework and Extra Credit Verification

This is to verify that _____ completed

_____ homework or _____ extra credit assignment on

_____   _____   _____
Date   Teacher   Course

Taking Charge

_____ 's Cumulative Points Record

Participant

_____

Session 1

    Group attendance _____   **Total** _____

Session 2

    Group attendance _____ School attendance _____

        Homework _____ Extra credits _____ **Total** _____

Session 3

    Group attendance _____ School attendance _____

        Homework _____ Extra credits _____ **Total** _____

Session 4

    Group attendance _____ School attendance _____

    Tasks _____ Homework _____ Extra credits _____ **Total** _____

Session 5

    Group attendance _____ School attendance _____

    Tasks _____ Homework _____ Extra credits _____ **Total** _____

Session 6

    Group attendance _____ School attendance _____

    Tasks _____ Homework _____ Extra credits _____ **Total** _____

Session 7

    Group attendance _____ School attendance _____

    Tasks _____ Homework _____ Extra credits _____ **Total** _____

Session 8

    Group attendance _____ School attendance _____

    Tasks _____ Homework _____ Extra credits _____ **Total** _____

        Grand total points _____

_____'s Points Earned as of Session _____

Participant Number

Group attendance _____ School attendance _____

Tasks _____ Homework _____ Extra credit assignments _____

Points earned this week: _____

Total points earned so far: _____

_____   _____
Group Leader   Date

_____'s **Points Earned as of Session** _____

Participant Number

Group attendance _____ School attendance _____

Tasks _____ Homework _____ Extra credit assignments _____

Points earned this week: _____

Total points earned so far: _____

_____   _____
Group Leader   Date

Taking Charge Group

Progress Notes

Session _____ Date _____

Leaders

Participants present

Activities of today's session

Strengths observed

Concerns

Overall progress toward skills mastery

Strategies for next session

_____   _____   _____   _____
Group Leader   Date   Group Leader   Date

Staffing Report

This form is for leaders' use in consulting with a supervisor or staffing the group with a treatment team.

Session _____   Date _____   Location _____

Leaders

What went well in this session:

Where we had trouble:

Where we would like consultation:

Chapter 4   *Leading the Taking Charge Group*

This chapter provides practical information on how to be an effective group leader and serves as additional training for those who wish to lead the Taking Charge groups. This training complements the practice manual that was presented in chapter 3. It may be of particular help to those who are new to leading groups, but more advanced group leaders will also find this chapter invaluable because it explains specific roles and functions of the Taking Charge group leader. Issues covered include the advantages of coleadership, managing group process, how to set up and manage the point system and incentives, how to do lunch, how to keep and manage records, effective training and teaching tips, and how to maintain intervention fidelity.

Coleadership

We recommend that the Taking Charge group curriculum be cofacilitated by two leaders. Many writers and researchers on group modality support coleadership for several important reasons:

- Coleaders achieve clearer, more informed perceptions of the group.

- Countertransference issues are more easily resolved with two leaders.

- When one leader is distracted or absent, the other one can take the lead.

- In sharing the load, coleaders experience less burnout.

When it is not possible to provide two leaders, we recommend that the designated leader identify a colleague or supervisor with whom to process the group experience after each session. This significantly reduces the sense of leader isolation and provides some compensation to the advantages of coleadership identified here.

Former Adolescent Mothers

It is desirable, though not essential, for one leader to have been an adolescent mother earlier in her life. This provides group participants with a strong social model. Clinical experience has also told us that current students who have finished one or more group programs and who are successful students may make excellent coleaders. Group members are likely to identify with a leader who shares their experience of adolescent pregnancy. They are likely to realize that they have the capability of succeeding in ways that she, a role model, has succeeded.

Training and Experience

The group is designed so that leaders are not required to have social work or related academic training, although prior experience leading groups and/or working with adolescents is an asset. BSW- and MSW-level social workers, graduate and undergraduate social work student interns, special education teachers, nurses, and school counselors have effectively facilitated the group. When the leaders are new to the profession or to school-based work or are volunteers, meeting with a supervisor or experienced practitioner at least weekly to process the group and receive feedback should be a priority.

Subgroups

At the point during group sessions when participants work on goals and tasks, leaders have a choice. Groups of 8 to 10 participants can remain together as one working unit. With a group larger than 10 participants, we recommend that leaders divide the group at this point, and each work with a smaller subgroup. We have observed that working in small subgroups facilitates more interaction among members as they work on goals and tasks. Many participants also need individualized attention from the leader when they are first learning how to do the worksheets. Younger participants or those who are otherwise limited in writing and cognitive skills may need consistent one-on-one help.

Feedback from group leaders as well as young mothers participating in the Taking Charge group, however, has been mixed on the pros and cons of dividing into subgroups. Therefore, our advice to leaders is to make a decision about this based on group's unique dynamics and needs.

Things to Remember About Group Process

A group's development usually happens in predictable stages: initial, transitional, working, and disengagement.

Initial Stage

When groups come together, the main task for participants is to develop trust. They must observe, interact, test, and evaluate to determine whether they can trust the leader and other members enough to risk becoming known to them. This may be particularly true for adolescents, although the fact that each participant has voluntarily agreed to be in this group may lessen the resistance. The main task for you as leader during this time is to *enable* a climate in the group in which trust can happen. Personal disclosure about yourself on whatever level feels comfortable for you, as the leader, is one way to help participants feel comfortable in beginning to disclose things about themselves. Another way that you can help create trust is to talk about confidentiality and protection of one another as group norms, or standards of behavior for the group.

Transition Stage

When the group has been going for a few sessions, the main task for participants is to develop less dependence on the leader and more dependence on themselves and other participants. They should begin to take responsibility for their own goals and to interact with one another in a mutually supportive, helpful way. Your leader function during this stage is to help create a group environment in which members can make these changes of deepening trust and interaction.

The leader's experience during this stage of group development can be the most challenging of all aspects of group leadership. In order for participants to reach a place of deeper trust, some degree of challenging one another, as well as their leader, will likely occur. As members are getting comfortable with their positions and roles in the group, conflicts may arise that are based on patterns of established behavior and previous relationships. Group members may not be aware of the underlying dynamics at the center of this discord. Adolescents, especially, may sincerely believe that they are experiencing feelings and reactions based on current, brand-new encounters. It is the leader's role to encourage the expression of feelings, feedback, and evaluation, as well as to offer some of their own feelings, observations, and interpretations. It is a good time for the leader to reinforce the group norm of talking about rather than acting out uncomfortable feelings with one another.

For the inexperienced leader or even for the leader with years of experience, the interactions during this stage may produce anxiety about whether or not the group is going to fall apart. The leader should not allow herself to make such an assumption. For most groups, this kind of testing is essential if participants are to move beyond the initial, guarded stage in which their deeper work has not yet begun. When open challenging and conflict begins to surface in the group, the leader should know that it is not because she has done something wrong. It is because, so far, she has probably done things right!

Working Stage

During this stage, members are facing genuine closeness with one another and a sense of bonding and interdependence. The leader's task is to encourage members to take the personal risks of self-disclosure and to give sincere feedback to one another that fosters intimacy. By this stage, the leader usually is becoming less directive and more a catalyst and supporter. Participants should feel basically safe with one another and with the group and should be moving ahead with their own work. Some leader functions at this stage may be to model here-and-now self-disclosure and feedback, to encourage contact and self-exploration among the group members, and to clarify positive and negative feelings.

Final Stage: Disengagement

Members must separate from the group and transfer their learning to life outside the group. Sometimes the group avoids the difficulty of termination by ignoring or denying their feelings about it, which is especially true of adolescents. The leader can help the group to keep this task in focus by calling attention to the upcoming termination several times, starting about 2 weeks before the actual end of the group. If the group's avoidance is extreme—for example, if more than usual are absent after termination is mentioned—the leader can talk with the group about their avoidance.

Another way the leader can help the group at this point is to talk about her own feelings about termination, which supports the benefits of experiencing and talking about separating and losing the group. She can encourage the group to evaluate their experience of the group—to organize into words the things they have gained from their participation and the things they will miss when it is over. Further, the leader can help link these ideas and feelings to future life outside the group and ways this learning experience will be transferred. The guides to Sessions 7 and 8 give specific directions for guiding the group through this phase. In the case of this group, most participants will continue to see one another often at school. The leader can help the group talk about how this contact with individuals whom they now know and trust can provide a continued source of support and feedback.

Incentives

To ensure that young mothers will receive the greatest benefit from Taking Charge by attending all sessions and carrying out assignments, incentives for attendance and other activities are built into the group. Incentives include food, a points system, and surprise gifts

Lunch Is Served

A chief incentive that participants immediately notice is food. Sharing food is a communal experience that enhances the social bonding we want to see in the group, and just as important, providing food gives a primal message of nurturance. Because group interventions such as Taking Charge are done in many schools during the lunch period, serving lunch during group is one such incentive. When the group does not meet during lunch, a snack should be provided. With limited time to accomplish the agenda in each session, it is important that lunch or snack be ready to eat when participants arrive. According to one 15-year-old Taking Charge participant, "Having lunch waiting for us was the best idea. It smelled so good when we came in the room, and we talked a lot while we ate [laughter]. It was a good time for me."

Points System

This incentive allows group members to earn points for group and school attendance, homework, extra credit assignments, and accomplished tasks toward an award gift at the end of Taking Charge. Awards should be something particularly attractive to participants, such as a gift certificate. When not enough points are earned for the top award, a second category for fewer points with a smaller award should also be included.

The Points System handout in chapter 4 suggests specific requirements for earning points. However, variations in school curriculums may call for designating point requirements that are compatible with the program. In some alternative school programs, for example, achievement is based on completion of learning units in the classroom rather than on homework and other traditional assignments. In instances such as this, points usually earned for homework and extra credit assignments must be awarded differently. Leaders inform participants about the points system during the first session and keep track of points each week, both for their own records and for participants.

Surprise Gifts

Twice during the group intervention (three times for a 12-week group) small surprise gifts are presented to every participant in attendance at the session. Besides providing encouragement to participate in every session, feedback from prior group leaders and young mothers says that this incentive is experienced as caring by group participants. In prior groups, gifts have included such items as hairbrushes and small manicure kits. A favorite with one group was spring equinox baskets made by their group leaders. Participants should receive these as the session is ending, given *only* to those in attendance at the designated session.

Why a Social Problem-Solving Process?

Adolescents can be very skilled at solving the kinds of problems they have confronted throughout childhood and adolescence. Negotiation and compromise, for example, are social skills that most adolescents have practiced since early childhood, since they first realized as toddlers that they had to get along with their siblings or first began school or day care. Bartering is a common social skill among adolescents (e.g., "I'll baby-sit your little brother on Sunday if you'll let me borrow your black dress on Saturday night"). They can demonstrate masterful skill at organizing social happenings with their friends and prioritizing their responses to school and parental demands, all without having to think much about what strategies they are using. These are skills they have developed over a long period of time by trial and error, through encouragement of their parents and other adults, and by observing older siblings and peers. They are skills that fit the demands of childhood and adolescence, and they have been supported and practiced for many years.

As we discussed in chapter 2, when an adolescent is confronted suddenly with the demands of parenthood, a set of new, unpracticed behaviors and skills are required. For perhaps the first time, the pregnant adolescent is without the stored knowledge and usual resources that may have served her to this point. She must learn how to consciously analyze her needs and problems, determine her goals, identify her resources, and devise ways to achieve what she needs. An important goal of Taking Charge is for participants to learn the process and application of solving their own problems instead of succumbing to becoming emotionally overwhelmed by them.

We believe that conscious social problem solving is an important life tool that accelerates developmental learning and enhances cognitive skills for coping with adult problems. Problem-solving skills have been found to be effective in helping adolescents with numerous behavioral problems and challenges, as we discussed in chapter 2. Adolescents seek autonomy and independence, and being able to competently solve their own problems helps them develop the sense of mastery that they need to accomplish goals that are likely to affect their life outcomes. Please refer to chapter 3 to examine the social problem-solving process used in Taking Charge.

Teaching the Social Problem-Solving Process

1. *Understand it.* The most important thing in teaching this process is to have a clear understanding of it for yourself. Occasionally, upon introduction to the Taking Charge curriculum, a leader has said something like, "Going through these steps is kind of silly. Everyone does this automatically." Although we fully agree that this is true for most

adults, in working through the steps of the process, group leaders often encounter difficulty mastering the process clearly enough to teach it to someone else. If we work through the process and discuss it with another person, we usually find that we are clearer about how to help our group participants do the same.

2. *Yield not to temptation.* We have observed and also heard from group leaders that one of the biggest temptations for leaders is to override member-identified goals and tasks that the leader judges to be unwise or destructive. The following story, illustrating this temptation, was reported at a focus group by one of the first Taking Charge group leaders.

We all did fine with the first goal, school achievement. It was the personal relationships goal where I had trouble. A 16-year-old member of the group was living with the family of her 22-year-old unemployed boyfriend and getting a lot of verbal abuse from him and from his mother. She declared that her relationship goal was getting her boyfriend to marry her! I was appalled, and I know it showed on my face. If our supervisor had not been in the back of the room observing that day, I'm sure I would have tried to have her change that goal. As it turned out, her task that week was to give her boyfriend an ultimatum about marriage. When she did this, his mother verbally attacked her for assuming that he would ever marry her. When her boyfriend was unwilling to defend his relationship with her and essentially elected to support his mother, the group member told us that she finally saw him clearly. She believes that particular task helped her to see that he could never be a good husband for her. She moved back home with her mother and is still there after the group ended 6 weeks ago. In the end, she knew more about what she needed to do than I did.

It is important to remember that we are teaching young mothers how to use this process as a *tool* that they feel comfortable with and will integrate into their ongoing social problem-solving and decision-making processes. When we attempt to infuse our own agendas and values into the participant's process, we risk losing her acceptance of the process as workable for her and taking ownership of her own outcomes.

3. *Repeat, repeat, repeat.* Taking Charge leaders tell us that many times they assume too soon that participants have mastered the

problem-solving process. They are disappointed when the group settles into forming goals and tasks for the second or third time and there is still confusion and misunderstanding. This excerpt from a focus group of leaders is typical of stories we have heard often:

We didn't want them to get bored with repetition, so we decided that we wouldn't go over the [problem-solving] steps with the group after the second session, unless they asked. During the third session we both worked with members that we thought would have a harder time with the steps, thinking that the others were getting on with their action plans. Near the end of session, I walked around the tables to check, and only one person had worked her action plan to the end! The others were doodling and talking to one another, and one was writing a letter. I felt like we wasted that entire session and almost lost the whole group. After that, we went over the steps every meeting just before we began on the action plans, and we kept an eye on every single member.

Managing Records and Documentation

Refer to the record-keeping forms in chapter 3 when reading this section.

Managing the Points System

For the points system to serve as a powerful incentive, it is important for members to be aware of how many points they have earned from week to week. An important tool in managing this record-keeping process is a file for each participant in which points documentation is stored. Placing a specific document into the participant's file for each points-earning activity reduces the likelihood of tallying errors and disputes over points. See box 4.1 for a list of these documents. School attendance documentation is accumulated during the week from school records, and group participants submit any other documentation at the beginning of each session. Pages 116–120 contain task, homework, and extra credit assignment forms, as well as individual and group points tally forms.

Box 4.1   **Documentation for the Points System**

Points-Earning Activity	Documentation Source
School attendance	School attendance records
Group attendance	Group sign-in sheet
Task completed	Task verification form
Homework	Homework verification form
Extra credit assignments	Extra credit verification form

Intervention Fidelity

Intervention fidelity means exactly what you would assume—staying true to the intervention as it is meant to be delivered. Rarely does a leader consciously intend *not* to present an intervention or a treatment as it is designed. It is subtle, seemingly unimportant changes and adaptations that occur during planning and presentation that can alter the treatment and change the process and outcomes. The Taking Charge practice manual in chapter 3 provides step-by-step directions for most important considerations, such as room setup and environment, leadership dialogue and style, timing, content, and process. Following the intervention manual in these aspects is central to achieving the expected outcomes from the group, especially directions for teaching the social problem-solving process and facilitating work on participant goals and tasks. For example, care should be given to avoid didactics on topics such as drug and alcohol use and prenatal care, except as participants may request information on these in developing their goals and tasks.

The following are some ways that leaders can ensure intervention fidelity in delivering the Taking Charge group curriculum:

- Read the practice manual. Read the practice manual carefully, perhaps more than once, to develop a comfortable sense of familiarity and understanding of the Taking Charge group curriculum.

- Work through the problem-solving process. In learning the intervention, work through the social problem-solving process in all four areas, identifying your own applicable goals and tasks. It is a complex set of skills, and you must first be good at it to teach the adolescent women.

- Discuss each session prior. Plan and discuss specific steps and content for each session with the coleader or a colleague prior to the session.

- Debrief each session afterward. Debrief with your coleader or a colleague after each session to identify ways that things may have "gotten off the track" and to plan for adjustments.

- Arrange for outside observation of sessions. Ask a colleague or supervisor who is familiar with Taking Charge group curriculum to observe several sessions and give feedback.

- Arrange to be trained by someone who has experience with the Taking Charge curriculum, when possible. Supervision and consultation of your initial work is also advisable, as was mentioned above. Research on intervention fidelity and learning how to apply evidenced-based practices suggests that the most effective way to learn an intervention is through direct training methods like workshops and in-service training, and the use of supervision and consultation models (Franklin & Hopson, 2007 in press). Please contact the authors to be advised of training opportunities on the Taking Charge group curriculum.

Summary

This chapter described practical information on how to be an effective group leader and served as additional training for those who wish to lead the Taking Charge groups. This training complements the practice manual that was presented in chapter 3. The chapter offered some foundational concepts in group training skills for individuals who need some basics in leading groups, as well as the more advanced skills that all leaders will need to be effective leaders of the Taking Charge groups. Issues covered include the advantages of coleadership, managing group process, how to set up and manage the point system and incentives, how to deal with lunch or snacks, how to keep and manage records, effective training and teaching tips, and how to maintain intervention fidelity.

Chapter 5   *Culturally Competent Leadership*

This chapter provides training for the leaders of the Taking Charge group curriculum and was meant to enhance the practice manual in chapter 3 and the training on effective group leadership in chapter 4. Culturally competent leadership is vital to the effectiveness of Taking Charge group curriculum with culturally diverse participants. We have said previously that one of the great strengths of the Taking Charge group curriculum is that it was found to be both effective and popular with immigrant and Mexican American populations and showed promise as an intervention that could help schools successfully span social class, race, and culture with pregnant and parenting adolescents.

This chapter covers essential knowledge and useful practice skills for making the Taking Charge groups culturally relevant for diverse participants. In particular, the chapter covers the cultural significance of language and dialect, rituals and activities, icons and metaphors, values, roles, and foods that represent *home*. Practice examples illustrate the importance of each of these elements and how they make the groups culturally competent and effective with adolescent mothers from diverse cultural backgrounds. We strongly advocate that group leaders develop culturally competent leadership by understanding the meaning of these cultural cornerstones for participants and further integrating them into the fabric of the groups that they lead.

Culturally Relevant Delivery

One of the most important dynamics associated with the effectiveness of this curriculum is the extent of its acceptance by young mothers. The group curriculum requires adolescent mothers to engage in new thinking and new behaviors, much of it between sessions when they are on their own without the guidance and support of the group. For this to happen, their *buy-in* to the curriculum must be substantial.

Educational and school support professionals such as school social workers, counselors, nurses, psychologists, and others know that for any educational intervention to be effective, these conditions must be achieved:

1. The student must have a clear understanding of the intervention.

2. The student must believe that the intervention can help her.

3. The student must have strong motivation to comply with the intervention.

Cultural relevance is fully as important as the leader's therapeutic and group leadership skills to assure that these three conditions are achieved. Although the fundamental processes of the group remain constant regardless of the group's cultural composition, the leader's style and the group's ambiance should be shaped by cultural considerations. The leader's knowledge of the group's cultural ecology (Koss-Chioino & Vargas, 1999) is *critical* to the group's receptivity of the intervention. Considering that the cognitive and behavior changes required by the curriculum are initially likely to feel alien and a bit daunting, the climate of the group should feel comfortable and familiar. It is careful consideration to culture that achieves this specific and valuable ambiance of *familiarity* in the group.

Respecting Cultural Values and Family Roles

Awareness of the cultural values that shape family and other social systems in the lives of group members is the starting point in a culturally relevant group experience. Not only are race and ethnicity to be considered, but also regional differences, education, employment and economic factors, and religious influences. The more differences between the leader and the group in these areas, the more imperative it is for the leader to become acquainted and comfortable with the values and social roles imprinted on young mothers in the group.

This can be a tricky business with young women in the adolescent stage of development in which deeply rooted family and cultural values are often being questioned and seemingly rejected. The wise group leader will understand that this rejection is part of the adolescent struggle for identity, and that the values of family and culture are still alive and well in the young mother's core value system. As such, the values do not necessarily need to be overtly recognized in the group, but they must be assumed and respected.

This can be further complicated working with adolescent immigrants in the process of acculturation to the United States, who may reflect a more mainstream cultural perspective in their school setting and peer group than they have truly internalized. Even though studies with immigrant adolescent mothers have shown that they are generally more assimilated than immigrant adolescents who have never been pregnant (Belcazar, Peterson, & Krull, 1997), leaders cannot safely assume that these young mothers have abandoned the requirements of their cultural roles as a daughter or family member. This group leader's experience with a young Vietnamese mother illustrates such a point:

The group had a discussion about problems in personal relationships on the day they worked on this goal. One of the most vocal members in the discussion said that her mother had just about taken over her baby. The group member worried that she could never be the mother to her child if something didn't change. I assumed that she would work toward confronting or at least talking to her mother about her concern, and made a comment about that to her. I later noticed that she had identified her goal but had not written any tasks for the week. When I asked what was going on, she said, "I couldn't do this the way you would do it. My family would turn their backs on me if I questioned my mother, and besides, that would change the way my mother is with me, forever."

Investigating family and other personal values of group members before the group begins is a good investment of the leader's time. This is especially so when the leader and the group are different from one another in important ways, or when the leader is new to the school and community. Here are some specific ways to conduct such an investigation:

- *Inquire of other professionals who work with these adolescents* what seems important to them about family, education, women's roles, religion, and other salient topics.

- *Investigate the community's attitudes* in these areas, as reflected by local political issues, the media, the school board, religious groups.

- *Investigate the education, religious preferences, occupational trends, and income levels* of the families in the community and specifically in your school.

- *Most important, talk to the young mothers in your school* and to their family members about these things.

Teaching Self-Sufficiency in the Context of Cultural Roles

Closely related to cultural values is the impact of cultural *roles*. The central theme of *self-sufficiency* in the Taking Charge curriculum relates to other concepts, such as *independence* and *autonomy,* that may appear to conflict with central values about women and family in some cultures. Unless this possible conflict is recognized and managed in a sensitive presentation of the curriculum, the result may be rejection by the young mother herself as well as by her significant others and family members. When the dominant culture values family unity and interdependence over autonomy and independence, these are some "frames" that can be introduced in teaching the fundamentals of the curriculum and leading group discussions around the four goal areas:

- *Self-sufficiency* can mean pulling one's own weight in the family, which is an asset to the family and beneficial to other family members. Have the group identify ways that their own self-sufficiency could benefit their family.

- *Independence* can be translated in many ways and is not synonymous with *separation*. Have the group define independence in the context of their families.

- *Autonomy,* being able to think for oneself, means that one can contribute meaningfully to the solving of family problems and be someone others in the family can look to.

As discussed, studies of minority adolescent mothers reveal that this population is less prone to follow conservative cultural values than adolescents who have never been pregnant. Nevertheless, adolescents are imprinted early with family and cultural values in ways that always impact their decisions and their lives. Expect that issues around self-sufficiency may create vigorous discussion and debate in the group. Make it a point to be supportive of all perspectives.

Cultural Metaphors and Icons

Parallel to understanding cultural values is being familiar with metaphors and icons that serve as cornerstones for culture. Mainstream American culture, for example, holds Betsy Ross as an icon associated with patriotism and the flag. In the Hispanic culture of the American Southwest, La Virgin de Guadalupe is a cultural icon associated with healing and hope for Protestants and nonbelievers, as well as Catholics, having expanded from a religious context into the broader cultural fabric. In teaching the problem-solving process and in helping the group to think and talk about education, relationships, parenting, and careers, the air of familiarity that encourages the group's receptivity is enriched when the leader can use stories and illustrations that are culturally familiar to group members.

Integrating the Dominant Language of Participants

In the best of situations, group leaders would be fluent in the dominant language of all participants. With the growing ranks of immigrant and refugee students whose first language is not English, this is most often not the case. Being able to recognize when participants are struggling to understand or communicate, and finding ways to exchange information across languages are important skills. Here are some strategies we recommend that may help leaders to bridge the language gap:

- *Learn and use some phrases in the second language,* such as "How's it going?" "Let's eat," "Can I help?" and "I don't speak [the language] very well!" You might ask group members who speak the other language to teach you. Even if you are not fluent, mastering a few language bytes tells the group that you recognize language differences and intend to support the language diversity of the group.

- *Invite group members to initiate discussions in their first language,* even if you do not understand much of what is being said. Above all, recognize that asking members who are not fluent in English to speak English exclusively in the group is counterproductive to their therapeutic experience. Group discussions in this curriculum are intended to expand participants' own thinking about their goals and problem-solving processes. Their capacity to fully engage in the exchange of thoughts and ideas is crucial to this process.

- *Occasionally ask one or more bilingual group members to translate for those who have difficulty understanding what you are saying* during portions of the group when you teach or explain in English. This can also be a good use of networking and can enhance supportive connections among group members. Be sensitive, however, to additional stress this may generate for the translating member as she is trying to engage her own thoughts and learning process.

- *Encourage members who are more comfortable in another language to do their written processes in that language.* It is probably more effective for you to have a colleague or the young mother herself translate the essential parts of the work for you, than for her to struggle with complex ideas in a language that she has not yet mastered.

Culturally Relevant Group Rituals

The way people get things done, including the way we deliver educational, social, and mental health services, is affected by culture. Group processes that educators, social workers, and other school practitioners accept as "the way it is supposed to be" were developed and have been followed in the context of someone's idea (bound by their own culture) of what is correct, appropriate, and effective. That cultural perspective may not be and is likely *not* to be, the most comfortable, understandable perspective of your group.

Across cultures, social groups come together in a variety of contexts based on roles and functions defined by characteristics such as gender, age, marital status, or religion. For example, in some Native American tribal groups, tribal governance is in the hands of elder males, whose strict assembly rituals are considered literally sacred and kept secret from those outside the group. In a less circumscribed but nevertheless essential group ritual, harvest time in many rural agricultural communities means that women of all ages gather to help with canning, freezing, and otherwise preserving the bounty in time to avoid spoilage and waste.

Rites of passage, such as birthdays, marriages, births, and deaths, carry diverse group rituals among cultures and within cultures. A baby shower in an African American community, for example, would traditionally be a gathering of female relatives and friends of the new mother. It would likely include light refreshments, a few games, some reminiscing with and about the young mother, opening gifts, and would likely be over in 2 to 3 hours. A baby shower in a Puerto Rican community, on the other hand, may be a gathering of entire families and close friends. It may include a full-sized meal with dishes contributed by the women guests and perhaps meat cooked by the men on an outdoor grill, informal visiting in lieu of organized games, children playing, teenagers coming and going, and would last all afternoon and into the evening.

The following story illustrates the importance of understanding culturally based rituals:

A social service center for women on the Texas border was requested by the public housing authority to provide therapeutic services at its large senior citizen complex. Many of the women living in the complex were showing serious signs of depression. In addition to individual therapy, the staff of the women's center decided to offer a group program that one of them had used effectively in the Midwest with older depressed clients. Focused on socializing older individuals, the program included weekly afternoons of table games, snacks, and outings.

The women's center program began with 25 Mexican American women, but by the third meeting there were only 9 women present. A focus group of women from the complex told the staff that most of the women felt "strange" playing card games and visiting places they had no reason to visit. They enjoyed visiting with one another during the meetings but felt distracted by the other activities. Further exploration revealed that the women missed activities such as cooking with other women and sharing meals with their families, making and sharing traditional holiday foods, and participating in the special occasions that marked the lives of them and their families.

With this feedback, the program was modified to include group meals prepared by the women themselves, developing a holiday cookbook of traditional Mexican recipes, planning and carrying out birthday and other special occasion parties for one another and other residents in the complex. Participation tripled, and within a few months the women told the staff that they would like to take responsibility for the group and move forward on their own.

What are the rituals of women in the dominant culture of your group? The rituals of adolescents? Of young mothers? How does preparing and sharing food feel to them? Do they prefer a bit of small talk before getting down to business? Knowing and incorporating social rituals that are similar to the ones people have participated in all their lives can help to provide reassurance and confidence in the face of new and unfamiliar experiences.

Case Illustration of Culturally Grounded Leadership With Five Mexican American Groups

All 73 young mothers who participated in the initial study of the Taking Charge group were Mexican American and Mexican immigrants. All except one coleader of the initial five groups were Mexican American and bilingual. The exception, who was Korean–African American, had lived on the U.S.–Mexico border much of her life and was familiar and comfortable with Mexican culture. This section describes some of the ways in which these leaders demonstrated cultural competency in facilitating the Taking Charge curriculum.

Language

Although Spanish was the first language of at least 80% of the group participants, leaders spoke English predominantly in conducting the group sessions. The main exception to this was when the group engaged in discussions on topics that aroused strong emotion, such as personal relationships. As well, leaders often spoke more in Spanish when they worked one-on-one with participants.

Once the groups were established, group members typically spoke with one another during the group in a region-specific English–Spanish style that incorporates both languages, sometimes informally referred to as *pocho* or *Spanglish*. For example, a group member was heard during one group session requesting of the person next to her, "Oye, por favor, pasame un pencil." To the uninformed observer, the lapse into this intimate, casual form of communicating has little social meaning, or may reflect ignorance of the languages. To the bicultural group leaders, it signaled that the young mothers were feeling comfortable with the group and making it their own experience.

One method for using language to inject culture was the use of Spanish sayings or *dichos*, even in groups in which English was the primary language and participants were totally bilingual. For example, one leader was observed using this dicho in a group discussion about relationships with boyfriends: "(Es bueno a) *decir mentiras para sacar verdades?*" Translated to English, this means, "(Is it okay to) tell lies in order to get at the truth?" Although this dicho translates reasonably well, sometimes an idea originating in one language can be difficult to replicate in another. More significantly, a dicho usually refers to a cultural truth that "hits home" most effectively in its original language.

Humor, Customs, and Acculturation

The use of culturally based humor, including stereotypical perceptions of men's and women's roles, and especially the food and recreational customs of people who live in the region, was woven throughout the delivery of the group. Leaders and participants often referred literally and metaphorically to food-related functions such as making tortillas, washing or cooking beans, and the *pico* (heat) of the chili. An example of this was overheard in one group during a discussion of school-related problems. A group member complained that no matter how much she changed her behavior and worked to be successful in a certain teacher's class, the teacher still treated her in the old way. As the leader and the young mother were exploring the value of having a heart-to-heart talk with the teacher to clear the air, another participant declared, "If you want a good pot of beans, you have to get the rocks out first."

A clearly present cultural reference in all the groups was the range of experiences associated with acculturation. Even for Latinos born and raised in the United States, being part of a cultural group in which immigration is an ever-present reality brings acculturation issues that affect their lives and are always with them. For example, most of the participants in these groups had relatives in Mexico, especially family elders, who impact their lives and the lives of their families in important ways. Experiences of visiting relatives in Mexico every holiday or during summer vacation, of *abuelitos* (grandparents) objecting to habits acquired in the United States by the acculturated grandchildren, and conflict with their own parents about social norms for American teenagers are some of the themes observed in group discussions.

Group Traditions

In choosing small gifts and forming group rituals, leaders used their knowledge of culture on several levels. In selecting small gifts instructed by the curriculum, for example, the leaders chose personal grooming items such as purse-size canisters of hairspray and small hairbrushes as the first gift, a reflection of their familiarity with the grooming preferences of Latina adolescents. In recognition of the strong religious holiday traditions of the border, they created Easter baskets for the young mothers as their second gift.

One group ritual that especially reflected the Mexican border culture was sharing food at every session. Lunch was always provided for participants, which they ate together while discussing their activities and tasks from the prior week. Occasionally there were snacks or desserts, such as *empanadas* and *biscochitos*, traditional Mexican pastries, prepared by participants or their mothers and served to the group. Every group followed tradition by having a cake to celebrate the group at the last session.

Another ritual was playing culturally familiar games at the beginning of some group sessions. One of these was a game called *Loteria* (Lottery), similar to bingo but with simple pictorial symbols rather than letters. Group leaders changed the symbols to fit various aspects of adolescence and parenting, such as a stroller, a schoolbook, a baby bottle, and a class ring. After this game was introduced at the fifth group session, some groups asked to play it every week. At one school, participants asked to borrow the game to play among themselves between sessions.

Summary

This chapter provided additional training for the leaders of the Taking Charge Group curriculum and was meant to enhance the practice manual in chapter 3 and the training on effective group leadership in chapter 4. Culturally competent leadership is vital to the effectiveness of Taking Charge group curriculum with culturally diverse participants. This chapter covered essential knowledge and useful practice skills for making the Taking Charge groups culturally relevant for diverse participants. In particular, the chapter discussed the cultural significance of language and dialect, rituals and activities, icons and metaphors, values, roles, and foods that represent *home*. The chapter strongly advocates that group leaders develop culturally competent leadership by understanding the meaning of these cultural cornerstones for participants and knowing how to integrate them into the fabric of the group.

Chapter 6 *Outcome Studies of the Taking Charge Group Intervention*

The Taking Charge group curriculum was constructed with the best evidenced-based research that we could find on adolescent motherhood. Outcome research on the Taking Charge group curriculum is ongoing. At the time of writing this book, three clinical studies have been completed on the Taking Charge group curriculum with a total of 139 young mothers. Pregnant and parenting students in three regular high schools, three alternative schools, and one dropout recovery program participated in the studies. Study 1 ($n = 73$) and Study 2 ($n = 46$) included multiple treatment groups, whereas Study 3 ($n = 19$) was done with one treatment group. This chapter discusses these three studies and their results. This chapter also reviews the results from qualitative data that we have collected from participants in the studies as well as participants in two Taking Charge groups that were not included in these studies. These case study and focus group data provide a wealth of information on the mothers' life experiences and how different aspects of the Taking Charge curriculum are significant to the mothers' progress. Several case studies are presented that illustrate this data.

About the Studies

The first and largest study was done in an urban school district on the U.S.-Mexico border. The study was conducted in response to school social workers who asked for a program intervention that would help reduce high absenteeism and failing grades among adolescent mothers in the district's 11 high schools. Taking Charge was developed by the authors during the following year, and district administrators agreed to a clinical trial in 5 high schools.

After this study found Taking Charge to be effective with a sample of Hispanic Mexican American teen mothers (Harris & Franklin, 2003), we wanted to test its effectiveness with young mothers of other cultural groups. Thus, the second study was done in an urban school district in northern Texas with a more culturally diverse student population. The sample in this study was comprised of African American, Anglo, Hispanic, and Asian American adolescent mothers.

In designing and conducting Study 2, we wanted to replicate Study 1 as much as possible. The two studies are alike in that they each had a treatment group and a control or comparison group, and each has the outcome variables of problem-focused coping, social problem solving, school attendance, and academic achievement. However, in addition to the cultural composition of the samples, several other differences are identified later.

Although the authors designed and directed the first two studies, the third study was designed and conducted by four graduate social work students in a semirural school district in New Mexico. The students and their field instructor sought permission from the alternative school where they were doing their field practicum to present the Taking Charge group and to test the group's effectiveness on the outcomes of school attendance and grades. The sample of young mothers in the study was 89% Hispanic and 11% Anglo (Harris, 2006, in review). We were interested in learning about the practitioner experience of developing as well as presenting the group in a school. We also wanted to learn what a third study would find about the group's effectiveness with school-related outcomes. Thus, the authors' primary involvement in the third study was to provide a 3-hour training with the 4 students and their field instructor, and to serve as consultants during the study.

Research Question and Outcome Variables

The question we asked in conducting the studies was whether Taking Charge would impact coping behaviors and social problem-solving skills that support school achievement, parenting, personal relationships, and employment/career. Studies 1 and 2 targeted these outcomes:

- Problem-focused coping behavior

- Social problem-solving skills

- School attendance

- School grades or academic achievement

Study 3 targeted only school attendance and academic achievement.

Study Participants

Study 1

Pregnant and parenting adolescent mothers in 5 high schools were invited to participate in the study. Young women who were pregnant up to their 8th month at the beginning of the study and those who had already given birth to a child whom they were parenting were eligible to participate. The 86 young women who entered the study were randomly assigned at their school to the Taking Charge group or to the control group. Those in the control group understood that they would have the opportunity to participate in Taking Charge the following semester. Four participants withdrew from the study before it began, and 9 dropped out of school during the course of the study. A total of 73 young women completed the study through posttest, 33 in the treatment group and 40 in the control group. All participants in the study self-identified as Mexican or Mexican American. They ranged in age from 14 to 20 and were in 9th through 12th grades.

Study 2

At the request of administrators at the alternative school where this study was conducted, all pregnant and parenting students enrolled at the school were invited to participate, with no eligibility restrictions. Forty-seven young mothers opted to participate in the study. Of these, 20 decided not to participate in the Taking Charge group but agreed to serve as members of the comparison group, whereas 27 decided to participate in Taking Charge and serve as the treatment group. After 1 student in the comparison group dropped out of school during the study, 19 remained in the comparison group and 27 in the treatment group at posttest. Of 46 participants, 19 were African American, 13 were Hispanic, 11 were Anglo, and 3 were Asian American. Participants ranged from 9th through 12th grades and in age from 15 to 19 (see table 6.1).

Table 6.1 Demographic Characteristics of Study Participants

	Study 1 n = 73		Study 2 n = 46		Study 3 n = 19	
	Treatment n = 33	Control n = 40	Treatment n = 27	Comparison n = 19	Treatment n = 12	Comparison n = 7
Age						
Mean	17.89	17.97	16.93	16.84	16.66	17.14
SD	1.44	1.39	1.38	1.11	2.32	1.53
Range	6.00	6.00	6.00	5.00	4.00	4.00
Grade in School						
9th	2 (6%)	4 (10%)	3 (11%)	3 (16%)	2 (17%)	1 (14%)
10th	8 (24%)	3 (8%)	2 (7%)	2 (11%)	5 (42%)	1 (14%)
11th	7 (21%)	14 (35%)	9 (33%)	6 (32%)	2 (17%)	2 (29%)
12th	16 (48%)	18 (45%)	13 (48%)	8 (42%)	3 (25%)	3 (43%)
Other	—	1 (2%)	—	—	—	—
Culture/Race						
Mexican American	26 (79%)	37 (93%)	4 (15%)	5 (26%)	10 (83%)	7 (100%)
Mexican citizen	5 (15%)	2 (5%)	—	—	—	—
African American	—	—	12 (44%)	5 (26%)	—	—
Asian American	—	—	2 (7%)	1 (5%)	—	—
Anglo American	—	—	8 (30%)	6 (32%)	2 (17%)	—
American Indian	—	—	—	2 (11%)		
Other	2 (6%)	1 (2%)	1 (4%)	—		
Parenting Status						
Pregnant	7 (21%)	10 (26%)	9 (33%)	4 (21%)	5 (42%)	3 (43%)
Have a child	24 (73%)	26 (67%)	13 (48%)	10 (53%)	4 (33%)	3 (43%)
Pregnant + child	2 (6%)	2 (5%)	5 (19%)	5 (26%)	3 (25%)	1 (14%)

Study 3

All pregnant and parenting mothers in this alternative high school were invited to participate in the study, and 23 accepted. Of these, 13 chose to participate in the Taking Charge treatment group, whereas 11 agreed to serve as the comparison group. During the study, 4 in the comparison group dropped out and 1 in the treatment group transferred to another school, leaving 12 in the treatment group and 7 in the comparison group at posttest. Seventeen participants self-identified as Hispanic or Mexican American, and 2 as Anglo. They ranged from 9th through 12th grades, and were 15 to 19 years old.

Study Designs

Study 1 used an equivalent groups design with random assignment to treatment and control. The 5 high schools selected to participate in the study were based on their larger numbers of teen mothers as well as the higher rates of school dropout among teen mothers in those schools. After completing a pretest, participants were randomly assigned to treatment or control group in each of the 5 schools. Those assigned to the control group received a $20 stipend for their participation at the end of the study and were invited to participate in a Taking Charge group the following semester.

Study 2 used a two-group quasi-experimental design. In following district policy, the principal at this alternative school requested that the participants not receiving the Taking Charge treatment be voluntary rather than assigned. Thus, in this study, the treatment group was composed of young women who chose to participate in the Taking Charge group, whereas the comparison group was composed of those who chose not to participate in the group.

Study 3 also used a quasi-experimental design. The social work interns conducting the study decided not to deny the Taking Charge group to any pregnant or parenting mother in the school. They invited those who chose not to participate in the Taking Charge group to participate in the comparison group. Seven participants thus became the comparison group, whereas 12 who chose to participate in the Taking Charge group became the treatment group.

Outcome Measures

In Study 1 and Study 2, a pretest and posttest were done to measure school attendance, academic progress, problem-focused coping, and social problem solving. In both studies, follow-up measures of attendance, problem-focused coping, and social problem solving were taken 6 weeks after the Taking Charge groups ended.

Study 3 measured attendance and grades for 6 weeks prior to beginning the Taking Charge group as pretest. The final 6 weeks of the Taking Charge group was the posttest period. Because the interns conducting the study graduated and left their program a month before the high school semester ended, a follow-up measure was not done.

In all three studies, attendance data was gathered from school records. In Studies 1 and 3, grades were measured from school grade records. In Study 2, the school measured academic progress by completion of course requirements. Thus, in that study, academic achievement was measured by the number of curriculum units completed by participants during the pretest and posttest periods. These were reported by classroom teachers.

In Studies 1 and 2, social problem solving was measured with the Social Problem-Solving Inventory-Revised, Short Form (SPSI-R), comprised of five items (D'Zurilla & Nezu, 1990). Problem-focused coping was measured with three subscales of the Adolescent Coping Orientation for Problem Experiences (A-COPE; McCubbin & Thompson, 1991). These subscales measured problem-focused coping behaviors in three domains: self-reliance, social support, and solving family problems. In both studies, the SPSI-R and the A-COPE were administered at 6-week intervals for pretest, posttest, and follow-up.

Study 1

Five Taking Charge groups were facilitated by school-based social workers, all women with BSW degrees. The groups were cofacilitated by young women who had become mothers during adolescence. The 10 leaders ranged in age between 21 and 33 years. Nine were Mexican American and bilingual, and 1 was Korean–African American and spoke only English. Young mothers were recruited as facilitators through day-care centers, the community college, and pediatric clinics. They were paid a stipend for each group session. Facilitators received 6 hours of training in 3-hour segments as a group, as well as 2 hours of training in dyads. Training was done by one of the authors, using the treatment manual found in chapter 3.

Study 2

Four Taking Charge groups participated in the study, each with two coleaders. The seven leaders, six Caucasians and one African American, were women between the ages of 25 and 51. A school social worker, school nurse, school counselor, special education teacher, and three graduate social work students served as leaders. The seven were trained in a group by one of the authors, in two 2-hour segments using the treatment manual as a guide.

Study 3

The Taking Charge group in this study was facilitated by two coleaders, both social work graduate students. One leader was Hispanic, age 25, and the other was Anglo, age 32. The two leaders were supervised by a licensed school social worker, although the supervisor did not work in the school where the study was conducted. Two graduate students who led the Taking Charge group and two others who designed the study and analyzed data were trained by one of the authors in a 3-hour session using the treatment manual as a guide.

Data Analysis

Equivalency of Groups

One way to help us reasonably assume that differences between the treatment group and control/comparison group at posttest were actually the result of Taking Charge was to determine whether the treatment group and the control/comparison group were equivalent at the beginning of the study. This was an especially important process for Studies 2 and 3 because the treatment and comparison groups were voluntary rather than randomly assigned. Group means were examined (see table 6.1), and a chi-square was calculated to examine equivalency between groups on categorical variables. An analysis of variance was calculated to examine the age of participants, pretest scores of the A-COPE and the SPSI-R (in Studies 1 and 2), school attendance, and GPA or academic progress. No significant differences between treatment and control/comparison groups were found at pretest (Harris & Franklin, 2003; Harris, 2006, in review). Therefore, on demographics and outcome variables, these three studies each began with two equivalent groups of young mothers.

Results

In both Study 1 (alpha .01) and Study 2 (alpha .05), a multivariate analysis of covariance found that the Taking Charge treatment had a significant overall effect at posttest, using pretest scores as covariates. In Study 1, the Pillai-Bartlett trace test for significance gave a value of .33 $(F = 7.20; df = 4,58; p < .000)$. Eta squared yielded a value of .33, indicating that 33% of the variance between the two groups was accounted for by the intervention (Harris & Franklin, 2003).

In Study 2, the Pillai-Bartlett Trace gave a value of .48 ($F = 7.84$; $df = 4$, 34; $p < .000$). The partial eta squared test produced a value of .48, signifying that 48% of the difference between the treatment and comparison groups was accounted for by the Taking Charge intervention (Harris & Franklin, 2006, in review).

In Study 3, the outcome variables of school attendance and GPA were each analyzed with an ANOVA rather than together with multivariate analysis. To help offset the possibility of a Type I error (false significance results), a Bonferroni adjustment was made, and alpha was set at .01.

Results on Outcome Variables

Problem-Solving Coping (A-COPE)

Studies 1 and 2 each identified problem-focused coping as an outcome variable and measured this variable with the A-COPE. In both studies, the treatment group made significant gain over the control/comparison group at the end of the Taking Charge intervention (see table 6.2).

Table 6.2 A-COPE Subscales Pretest, Posttest, and Follow-Up Means and Standard Deviations

	Study 1		Study 2	
	Treatment	*Control*	*Treatment*	*Comparison*
Pretest				
Mean	58.52	58.35	53.88	57.58
SD	10.41	9.05	9.03	7.04
Posttest				
Mean	65.58	56.85	61.48	55.58
SD	10.47	11.09	8.42	7.61
Follow-up				
Mean	64.07	56.62	59.37	56.21
SD	9.57	12.55	7.78	6.50

Study 1 ANOVA results: $F = 15.98$; $df = 1,70$; $p < .000$; eta squared $= .19$. Study 2 ANOVA results: $F = 24.47$; $df = 1,43$; $p < .000$; eta squared $= .36$.

In Study 1, the treatment and control group A-COPE scores were almost identical at pretest (treatment = 58.52; control = 58.35). At posttest, the control group score was lower (56.85), whereas the treatment group score had increased by 7 points (65.58).

In Study 2, the comparison group's pretest score on the A-COPE (57.58) was nearly 4 points higher than the treatment group score (53.88). At posttest, the treatment group had gained nearly 8 points (61.48), whereas the comparison group lost 2 points (55.58).

Social Problem Solving (SPSI-R Short Form)

Social problem solving was measured in Studies 1 and 2 with the SPSI-R Short Form. The maximum possible score on this scale is 20 points. At posttest in each study, the treatment group score was significantly higher than the control or comparison group score (see table 6.3).

In Study 1, the treatment group score and control group score were nearly identical at pretest (treatment = 12.88; control = 12.98). At posttest, the treatment group score (14.94) was 2.08 points higher, whereas the control group score (12.08) dropped almost 1 point.

In Study 2, there was a 0.83-point difference between the treatment group pretest score (12.53) and the comparison group score (11.70).

Table 6.3 SPSI-R Short Form Pretest, Posttest, and Follow-Up Means and Standard Deviations

	Study 1		Study 2	
	Treatment	*Control*	*Treatment*	*Comparison*
Pretest				
Mean	12.88	12.98	12.53	11.70
SD	3.14	2.85	3.71	3.94
Posttest				
Mean	14.94	12.08	13.92	11.35
SD	3.17	2.86	3.26	3.88
Follow-up				
Mean	14.93	12.88	13.46	11.00
SD	3.56	3.43	2.56	3.69

Study 1 ANOVA results: $F = 19.49$; $df = 1.70$; $p < .000$; eta squared = .22. Study 2 ANOVA results: $F = 5.48$; $df = 1,41$; $p < .024$; partial eta squared = .29.

At posttest, the treatment group score (13.92) had increased by 1.39 points, whereas the comparison group score (11.35) had decreased slightly.

School Attendance

School attendance in all three studies was defined as the percentage of days that the participant attended school. In all three studies, the treatment group at posttest had a significantly higher percentage of school attendance than the treatment group (see table 6.4).

In Study 1, the treatment group (.83) and control group (.84) were nearly identical in their school attendance at pretest, both groups having missed an average of about 5 days of school during the previous 6 weeks. At posttest, the treatment group (.90), with a 7% increase in school attendance, had missed an average of only 3 days of school compared to the control group (.83), which had dropped 1% in attendance and had again averaged about 5 days missed over the previous 6 weeks.

At the beginning of Study 2, the treatment group (.78) had missed an average of about 7 days of school during the previous 6 weeks, and the comparison group (.81) had missed an average of about 6 days. At

Table 6.4 School Attendance (Percent) Pretest, Posttest, and Follow-Up Means and Standard Deviations

	Study 1		Study 2		Study 3	
	Treatment	Control	Treatment	Comparison	Treatment	Comparison
Pretest						
Mean	.83	.84	.78	.81	.80	.80
SD	.14	.17	.14	.11	.08	.16
Posttest						
Mean	.90	.83	.86	.77	.88	.78
SD	.01	.15	.12	.20	.06	.14
Follow-up						
Mean	.86	.75	.86	.75	—	—
SD	.12	.20	.14	.21	—	—

Study 1 ANOVA results: $F = 9.791$; $df = 1,70$; $p < .003$; eta squared $= .12$. Study 2 ANOVA results: $F = 5.373$; $df = 1,43$; $p < .025$; partial eta squared $= .11$. Study 3 ANOVA results: $F = 15.178$; $df = 1,16$; $p < .001$; partial eta squared $= .49$.

posttest, the treatment group, with an increase in attendance to 86%, had missed school an average of about 3½ days the previous 6 weeks, whereas the comparison group, with a drop in attendance to 77% at posttest, had missed an average of about 7 days during the previous 6 weeks.

In Study 3, the treatment group (.80) and comparison group (.80) were identical in attendance at pretest, each group having missed about 6 days of school during the previous 6 weeks. At posttest, the treatment group (.88), with an 8% increase in attendance, had missed about 3½ days over the previous 6 weeks, compared to the comparison group (.78) with a 2% drop in attendance and about 6½ days missed over the previous 6 weeks.

Grades/Academic Achievement

Academic achievement in Studies 1 and 3 was defined by the participant's grade point average (GPA) and measured with data from school grading period records. In Study 2, academic achievement was defined as the number of curriculum packets completed by the participant and was measured with data reported from classroom teachers. In all three studies, the treatment group made significant gains in academic achievement at posttest compared to the control/comparison group (see table 6.5).

Table 6.5 Academic Achievement Pretest and Posttest Means and Standard Deviations

	Study 1 GPA		Study 2 Curriculum Units		Study 3 GPA	
	Treatment	Control	Treatment	Comparison	Treatment	Comparison
Pretest						
Mean	77.84	77.45	7.26	8.00	80.62	83.43
SD	9.52	7.89	5.77	3.74	4.95	7.19
Posttest						
Mean	79.59	71.63	12.44	8.58	82.66	80.73
SD	11.03	16.48	8.72	3.89	4.34	9.48

Study 1 ANOVA results: $F = 7.07$; $df = 1,64$; $p < .010$; eta squared $= .10$. Study 2 ANOVA results: $F = 21.66$; $df = 1,43$; $p < .000$; eta squared $= .34$. Study 3 ANOVA results: $F = 25.625$; $df = 1,16$; $p < .000$; partial eta squared $= .62$.

Taking Charge

At the beginning of Study 1, the treatment group GPA (78.75) was nearly identical to the control group GPA (78.52); both classified as a C average. At posttest nine weeks later, the treatment group had gained over two points (80.79), rising from a C average to a B average. This was significantly higher than the posttest control group GPA (72.63), which had lost nearly 6 points, dropping from a C average to a D average.

In Study 2, for the 6-week pretest period, the treatment group score (7.26) for the number of academic units completed was slightly lower than the comparison group (8.00). At posttest 6 weeks later, the treatment group (12.44) had gained nearly 5 points, significantly surpassing the comparison group (8.58), which had remained about the same as at pretest.

For the 6-week pretest period at the beginning of Study 3, the treatment group GPA (80.62) was lower than the comparison group GPA (83.43) by 2.81 points. At posttest 6 weeks later, the treatment group (82.66) had gained 2.04 points in GPA, surpassing the comparison group GPA (80.73), which had dropped by 2.70 points.

Follow-Up Results

In considering the lasting value of the Taking Charge group for young mothers, we were interested in the long-term effects. Thus, in Studies 1 and 2, a follow-up measure was done 6 weeks after the Taking Charge groups ended to examine whether the beneficial changes in the treatment group had lasted. Analysis done on school attendance, problem-focused coping, and problem-solving skills (follow-up data was unavailable for grades) showed that in both studies the significant differences between the treatment group and the control group found at posttest still held after 6 weeks (see tables 6.2–6.4).

Implications for School Dropout

Although whether the Taking Charge group had an impact on school drop-out rates was not identified as a separate outcome in these studies, our preliminary results on this continuing problem for teen mothers should be reported. In Study 1, of 86 students who initially entered the study, 8 students in the control group (20%) dropped out of school during or after the study, compared to 1 student in the treatment group (3%). Of 46 students who entered Study 2, 3 comparison group participants (16%) dropped out of school during the study, whereas 100% of participants in the treatment group remained in school until the end of the school year.

Participant Goals and Tasks

We reviewed goals and tasks in all four domains for 78 to 81 teen mothers in Taking Charge groups, as well as written reports from leaders and results from three focus groups with Taking Charge leaders and participants. This section presents the dominant themes we found in the goals and tasks. We have also included de-identified case examples from Taking Charge leaders, as well as focus group comments from leaders and participants about their experiences with Taking Charge.

School Achievement Goals and Tasks

The sources identified above support much of what other research tells us about teen mothers and academic struggle. The three dominant school concerns identified by participants (see table 6.6) and leaders in the Taking Charge groups we have studied are related to attendance, grades,

Table 6.6 School Goals and Barriers of 81 Taking Charge Participants

Increase Attendance (53 participants)	Improve Grades (18 participants)	Increase Motivation (12 participants)
■ No child care	■ Lack of time to study	■ Feel lonely at school
■ Baby health issues	■ Need academic help	■ Feel embarrassed
■ Family pressure	■ Conflict with teacher	■ Feel sad and depressed
■ Conflict at school		■ No longer see benefit
■ Tired and depressed		

and motivation. Each of these interrelate with the other two to such a degree that it was often difficult to separate the three.

Attendance

As indicated by 81 participants on their problem-solving worksheets, 53 (65%) identified missing too many days of school as the main obstacle in achieving their school goals (see table 6.6). Twenty-seven (33%) cited irregular or unaffordable child care as the main reason for school absences, 11 (13%) identified their or their baby's recurring illnesses or health problems, 8 (10%) described conflicts with family members or baby's father that often left them without transportation or child care, and 4 (5%) cited relationship issues with friends or teachers. Three (4%) wrote that often they were too tired or depressed to go to school. In examining these reasons for missing days of school, it is clear how interrelated parenting, personal relationships, and economic well-being are with a young mother's chance of being successful with school.

Claudia

Claudia was a 16-year-old junior with a 4-month-old son when she began participating in the Taking Charge group at her school. When the group began working on school goals, Claudia confided to the group that she was afraid she was going to fail her junior year. She had missed more school since her son's birth than the previous 2 years of school combined. Claudia's older sister took care of Alex most days, but Claudia had to stay home with him whenever her sister was needed to drive their grandmother or her sister to medical or other appointments. Recently their grandmother had had complications from diabetes, and Claudia was missing 1 or 2 days of school each week.

In listing possible strategies for increasing her attendance, Claudia considered these three: (1) asking her best friend's mother to pinch hit for child care, (2) finding someone else in the family who would take care of Alex on days when her sister was not available, and (3) applying for subsidized day care at a center near school that her counselor had told her about. She told the group that she had never visited a day-care center and that her family believed in family members taking care of their children. As she explored her options, however, the day-care center near school seemed most dependable and appealing to her. Claudia made her first task to visit the child-care center and talk to the director and child-care staff to see for herself what it was like. Her second task was to have a frank talk with her mother about missing so much school and what she was considering, asking for her mother's support. Claudia told her leader that she hardly ever initiated conversations like this with her mother, and she was nervous about trying it.

The following week in session, Claudia reported that she had been afraid to go to the day-care center alone, so she had taken her best friend with her and they both liked what they saw. When she approached her mother about the day-care center, she was shocked when her mother agreed with her and said she would have suggested a day-care center herself earlier, except that she thought Claudia would "feel bad about the idea." The day before group, Claudia had completed a third task—returning to the day-care center with her mother and sister and registering her baby to begin the following week.

Grades

Of the 81 goals that we reviewed, 18 (22%) identified improving grades as their school-related goal (see table 6.6). Nine (11%) cited lack of time to complete homework, do assignments, and study for tests. Six (7%) wrote that they have difficulty understanding the material and need extra help with various courses. Three (4%) identified conflict or lack of communication with teacher or counselor.

Ana

Ana was a 17-year-old senior, 5 months pregnant when she began the Taking Charge group. She was a vivacious, outgoing young woman who talked and laughed a lot in group and was usually in the center of activity. In identifying her goal for education, Ana said she wanted to graduate in May and go to cosmetology school the next year. However, she was worried that she was going to fail a required class that she had fallen behind in this semester. She was concerned that she would not be able to catch up, especially because she would have to miss a few days when her baby was born before the end of the semester.

Ana said the main barrier to passing this class was that the teacher did not like her or take her seriously. She said the teacher did not talk to her or include her in class discussions, especially because it had become clear that she was pregnant. Ana responded by sitting in the back of the room, saying as little as possible, and leaving immediately after class.

It was difficult for Ana to find strategies for passing the class without exploring ways to communicate with her teacher. She was reluctant to engage in what she described as "chitchat" with a teacher, whom she believed did not like or respect her. Although she gave herself the task of having a friendly conversation with her teacher during the week of school-related tasks, Ana was unable to carry it out. What she was able to do, which ultimately turned things around with her teacher, was to begin asking for extra credit assignments and for her teacher to sign verifications every time she turned in homework.

In the final group session, Ana said that she had first begun asking for extra credit assignments just to earn extra points for the gift certificate award. But as she and her teacher began to talk about the assignments and Ana felt more confident, she looked forward to working on extra assignments and discussing them with her teacher. At the last Taking Charge session when participants were sharing high points of their experience, Ana announced that her previously "problematic" teacher had nominated her for an end-of-year award.

Motivation

We discovered several reasons that participants gave for missing too much school due to lack of motivation. We classified the issue as *motivation* when participants were clear that they simply did not want to attend or participate in school on many days. Twelve participants (15%) identified school goals related to motivation. It is interesting to note that 10 of these group participants were younger than 16, and 9 of them were in the 9th grade. Of the 12, 5 participants (6%) described a goal of finding friends or a new sense of connection at school. Four (5%) said that on many days they could no longer see any benefit to them for continuing in school. Three participants (4%) identified goals related to feeling better about their lives in general. As one stated in her worksheet,

"[My goal is] to start feeling better so I can get up and go to school and where I used to go."

Parenting Goals and Tasks

The Taking Charge curriculum provides a forum for young mothers to identify and explore the aspects of parenting that are problematic for them. A review of 78 parenting goals and focus group feedback from leaders and participants yielded results that parallel issues identified in other research, as well as some that are surprising (see table 6.7). We were perhaps most interested to note how often parenting goals and tasks spilled over into other life domains, especially personal relationships.

Table 6.7 Parenting Goals and Barriers of 78 Taking Charge Participants

Number of Participants	Goal	Barrier(s)	Reasons for barrier(s)
31	A stronger mothering role or relationship	■ Others take care of baby more than mother does ■ Mother lacks skills	■ Little time with baby ■ Grandmother competes ■ Others demean mother's efforts
28	A better coparenting relationship with baby's father	■ Disagreements or disengagement with father and father's family	■ Conflict with father's mother ■ Lack of financial help ■ Lack of father help or involvement ■ Families competing for baby
19	Better day care, health care, and other baby resources	■ Communicating needs to providers ■ Do not know resources ■ Limited choices due to cost	■ Do not know what questions to ask or when to disagree ■ Intimidated by experts ■ Providers "on the list" are not good

The 78 participant goals that we reviewed (see table 6.7) were clustered fairly evenly into three themes: (1) 31 goals (40%) had some aspect of assuming a stronger parenting role with their baby; (2) 27 goals (35%) related to coparenting with the baby's father and his family; (3) 19 goals (24%) focused on dealing with child care, health care, and other resources related to the baby's care.

Most young mothers who identified the goal of being a stronger mother lived with their own mother or with the family of their baby's father. Self-identified barriers to the goal reflected the young mother feeling pressured by other family members to strengthen her mothering role, and/or distress from the notion of being replaced by the baby's grandmother or child-care provider. We selected the following story of one participant and her task plan and report as one of numerous similar experiences.

Carol

Carol was 17 and a junior when she participated in Taking Charge. She and her 2-year-old daughter, Julia, lived with her parents and two older brothers. Carol said in her Taking Charge group that she had been happy and relieved to have her mother take charge of things when Julia was born. At 15, Carol knew little about babies and was even afraid to hold Julia in the beginning. Carol's mother made decisions about formula and diapers and got up in the night for Julia's feedings. Carol learned to feed, bathe, and play with the baby by observing her mother. Carol's parents bought all of Julia's diapers, clothing, and food, and they often took her with them when shopping and visiting friends or relatives. Carol said she was happy during Julia's first year, that her parents gave Carol so much freedom, and that they took such good care of the baby. Only in the past year had Carol begun to feel the sting of her own mother being more like Julia's mother than she was. Although she and Julia were close, Julia showed a clear preference for Carol's mother, especially when she was tired or sick. Carol's mother, for her part, was not consciously possessive of Julia but definitely had the last word on decisions about the child. Carol had become more and more disturbed about this situation but felt unable to change things. She did not want to hurt her mother or make her parents think that she was ungrateful for all the help they had given her with Julia.

As she explored her parenting role in the group, Carol concluded that she must spend more time with Julia in order to make herself a primary figure to the child. She made having a strong mother-child relationship with her daughter her parenting goal. She selected the strategy of working with Julia on developmental accomplishments such as toilet training and learning new words. One of her tasks was to work with Julia on toilet training during the week between sessions. This is Carol's task planner and task report:

Task Planner

First Task for <u>Carol</u>   Parenting

Group member   Goal area

Strategy: Be the one who teaches Julia how to go potty.

Description of task   Work with Julia on learning how to go potty this week.

What I will do to accomplish this task:

I will buy pull-ups and tell her what they are for on Saturday morning. I will put them on her, and take her to the bathroom. I will spend 15 or 20 minutes in the bathroom with her just playing and trying out the potty chair. I will take her to the potty chair two or three times during the day and before bath time.

I will do this by <u>4/7</u>, **and I will ask** <u>my mother</u> **for help if I need it.**

Date _____   Helper _____

What Happened to My First Task

I (did) <u>X</u> (did not) __ get this task done this week. This is what happened:

Just before bath time Saturday my baby went potty in her potty chair. She has gone potty in the chair with me in the bathroom three times since then—Sunday afternoon, Monday evening, and today. The time with just me and her is working.

My evidence that I completed this task is:

She went.

This is what I plan to do next:

Buy more pull-ups and keep taking Julia potty.

Intermingling of Life Domains Reflected in Goals

The second cluster of goals, associated with coparenting with the baby's father, was also present in relationship goals, although the goals in parenting were centered more specifically on parental functions than on other aspects of the relationship between young mother and father of the baby (see table 6.7).

These focus group statements from two participants reflect a theme that we have encountered often:

- "In my mind, I combined the goals of relationships and parenting. I put them together because my relationship with my husband and his family affects my daughter."

- "Parenting and relationship linked up together for me. I live with my baby's daddy, his parents, our baby, and his two nieces. My relationship goal with his mom also affected parenting stuff and helped me to get my baby into day care."

Thirteen goals, nearly half of this cluster, reflected issues of managing the mother's and father's larger family systems in coparenting their child.

The cluster of goals related to dealing with systems and professionals around the baby's care and development was unexpected. Eleven of these young mothers, more than half, lived with the father of their baby in a separate household from any family, which may suggest less guidance from older family members in selecting, arranging, and communicating with child-care and health-care systems and providers. Seven of the group were age 16 and younger, which may also suggest lack of practice as an adult consumer dealing with professional systems.

Career/Employment Goals and Tasks

We observed the career- and employment-related goals of 79 Taking Charge participants (see table 6.8). These goals, along with reports from group leaders, suggested that many young women who participated in

---

Taking Charge had not thought to any significant degree about their economic future. A substantial number, especially younger participants, did not see themselves as serious wage-earners prior to participating in the group. Career-related goals varied by age and grade in school more than goals in other life domains. Leaders observed that younger participants, such as those in 9th and 10th grades, were less interested in this area than others, whereas some older participants, especially those who were seniors, engaged with this goal more energetically. Focus group comments such as the following help to explain this variation in responses to career-planning as a goal:

Participant (sophomore, age 16):   Career was the least goal for me. My task of looking up jobs that are most available and that make a lot of money was kind of a trip, really. But I have too much else to worry about besides a career until I'm ready to graduate.

Group leader: We noticed how the older girls in our group grabbed onto the career goal. Something like career planning takes on new meaning when they get to work it through like they did (in group)—it's an immediate concern for them, and this took it from something other people do, to something *really possible for them.*

Regarding their attitudes and beliefs about employment and careers, four clusters of participants were described by leaders: (1) participants, most of whom were 16 and younger, who believed they would be supported by their family or the father of their baby and would not need

Table 6.8 Career and Employment Goals of 79 Taking Charge Participants

Number of Participants	Goal	Barrier(s)	Reasons for Barrier(s)
57	Make a career choice and plans before high school graduation	Lack of knowledge about career choices	Have not thought about this or investigated
20	Enter college or trade school after graduation	■ Have not applied ■ Financial resources	■ Not a priority ■ Family can't afford
2	Work in current part-time job and begin college	Financial resources	Lack of money to go to college full-time

to be employed; (2) participants who assumed that they would eventually work in some kind of job just to add to the household, but had no preferences or plans; (3) participants who had some, often vague, idea of a career they wanted to pursue, but had not become informed or taken any steps; and (4) participants who were in various stages of planning for their chosen career.

Of the 79 Taking Charge participant goals we reviewed, only 22 showed prior decisions about employment or a career. With two exceptions, these participants were 17 or older and seniors in high school. Two of this group already had part-time jobs that they planned to continue in after graduation, one as law firm clerk and the other as a grocery store cashier. Both also planned to begin college part-time. Most of these 22 identified goals that involved further training or education, such as technical schools (business, cosmetology, culinary art, welding) upon high school graduation. Four identified professional career goals, including journalism, law, nursing, and social work. Tasks identified in this cluster ranged from researching available schools to gathering application materials, submitting applications, researching and applying for financial aid and scholarships, and interviewing with schools.

Goals of the remaining 57 showed that they were only beginning or had not thought about future employment or a career. Most of their goals were linked to making a career choice, with strategies around learning about various career fields. The tasks they chose were such activities as speaking with their school counselor about various job fields, researching careers in the school library or on the web, participating in the school job fair, and interviewing someone with a job that looked interesting to them.

Feedback from leaders suggests that participating in Taking Charge and thinking about employment and a career in the course of working on this goal had an important impact on a number of the young women. Although some, specifically those 15 and younger with some years until high school graduation, continued to see the career goal as a sort of fantasy, others began to examine new possibilities during group discussions and as a result of their tasks. The following case vignette is one example of participant experiences with this goal area while participating in Taking Charge. This young mother's experience demonstrates once again how inextricably education and career planning are linked.

Juana

Two months short of turning 19, Juana was a senior when she entered the Taking Charge group spring semester. Juana had two children, ages 3 and 2, and had married the father of her children the previous semester. Juana's family had emigrated from Mexico when she was 12. Two years later, her mother had returned to Mexico, leaving Juana with her father and two younger siblings. Juana had continued to live with her father and siblings through the births of her own two children while her boyfriend graduated from high school and worked as apprentice to an electrician. The previous summer, Juana's father had died in an accident. Juana and her boyfriend had married and established a household that included their two children as well as Juana's 14-year-old brother and 16-year-old sister.

When she began the Taking Charge group, Juana was distraught at having been told recently by her school counselor that she would be two courses short for graduating in the spring as she had planned. She was considering dropping out at the end of the semester and getting a GED. She had decided that at her age, her new family took precedence over staying in high school another semester, when she should be working or learning a trade. Juana's Taking Charge group encouraged her to get the two courses done during the current semester and graduate as she had planned. Another group member had taken nontraditional classes to make up courses and told Juana about some options. Still not sure she could manage it, Juana gave herself the task of talking to her counselor about ways to take the two additional courses that semester.

The following week, Juana had enrolled in a night class at the technical high school as well as a flexible hours class in the district's dropout recovery program. In her class at the technical high school, Juana met students who were attending a business college with classes on the tech high school campus. Her career goal later in the Taking Charge group was to enter a training program at that school after high school graduation. Two weeks after the Taking Charge group ended, Juana learned that she was accepted with a full scholarship to a 6-month program to become a court translator and stenographer.

Although younger participants in most of the Taking Charge groups engaged less with career goals than other goals, there were notable exceptions. The following is an example of stories reported by group leaders about younger participants.

Andrea

At age 16, Andrea was the youngest of three sisters and the second to become pregnant in high school. Although Andrea was a strong student and had made good grades throughout school, especially in science and math, it was clear to her group leaders that she had not thought about a career. Andrea said she always thought she would work in a clothing plant like her mother and aunt, or maybe a merchandise warehouse like her older sister.

When her Taking Charge group began working on the career goal, Andrea learned that one of the older members wanted to enter college the following year to become a nurse. Another senior was already working part time in a law office and wanted to become a court reporter. Andrea was amazed when she heard the others talking about the salaries they could earn in these professions. She wrote down as her goal to enter college or training for a career by the time she graduated from high school. Because her knowledge about careers she might want to consider was vague, as her task for the following week she took finding out about careers in her favorite subjects, biology and accounting. This is Andrea's task report:

What Happened to My Task

I (did) X (did not) __ get this task accomplished this week. This is what happened:

I looked on the computer in the library for different careers in biology that you can get trained for at the community college. I found at least six before I had to leave. They're all medical jobs. I found out you can get trained and go to work in three of them in 6 months.

My evidence that I completed this task is:

Mrs. Raymond (librarian) helped me find the community college on the web and pick out the links to what I wanted. She signed my task sheet.

This is what I plan to do next:

Mrs. Raymond said I should call and ask the community college to send more information and talk to one of their counselors about financial aid. I probably will do that.

Relationship Goals and Tasks

As Taking Charge group participants identified relationship goals in their personal support systems, leaders repeatedly observed how disruptive pregnancy and childbirth were to relationships across group members' lives. Leaders in both focus groups agreed that of the four goals, their groups responded most energetically to the relationship goal. According to one leader, "When we started our relationship discussion, it was like an explosion in our group. I thought they would never finish talking and get to work on their written goals."

Although participants were perhaps no more productive with goals and tasks in this area than in others, some accomplished major changes such as leaving abusive living situations and challenging abusive parents or boyfriends. Our analysis of 78 relationship goals support several research conclusions discussed in chapter 1 (see table 6.9). Of 78 goals, 41 (53%) identified the mother-daughter relationship, 27 (35%) identified their relationship with boyfriend or baby's father, and 10 (13%) identified relationships with friends or other family members. In most cases, relationship difficulties were related directly or indirectly to the

Table 6.9 Relationship Goals of 78 Taking Charge Participants

Number of Participants	Goal	Barrier(s)	Reasons for Barrier(s)
41	Improve relationship with mother or boyfriend's mother	■ Argue a lot ■ Don't communicate ■ Baby's needs ■ Mother's friends ■ Family differences	■ Mother too strict ■ Expects too much ■ Critical of baby's care ■ Argue about boyfriend ■ Can't agree on things
27	Improve relationship with boyfriend or baby's father	■ Argue all the time ■ Little time together ■ Families interfere ■ Friends interfere	■ Doesn't help with baby ■ Doesn't give money ■ Goes out with friends ■ Not attentive
10	Improve relationship with sibling, friend, or other relative	■ Conflicted ■ or distant relationship	■ Sibling jealousy ■ Friend has no time ■ Friend, father, sibling, cousin feels left out

participant's pregnancy or birth of a child. From our observations, these are some themes of impact on personal relationships:

1. The most problematic relationships for young mothers are with their own mother and with the baby's father.

2. Young mothers continue to need their mother's approval and care, and are motivated to accommodate to that relationship.

3. Differences in parenting involvement, priorities, and social activities for the young mother and young father contribute most often to conflict in their relationship.

4. The birth of a teen mother's baby draws family members from both sides, especially grandmothers, into interactions with the young mother that are often perceived by her as judgmental, rejecting, or competitive.

5. Baby's entry into the family system can threaten established family structure and roles, contributing to relationship conflicts with siblings and others in the household.

6. Peer relationships often change, and although they not as often a priority issue as family and boyfriend relationships, many of these changes are a source of stress.

Participant goals and experiences were varied in the domain of personal relationships. Just as with the domain of education, relationships for these young mothers are interdependent with other domains, especially parenting. The following case vignette reflects such interdependence.

Martha

Martha was 16 and a junior when she participated in Taking Charge. She was talented in art and planned to major in commercial art at the community college after high school. Martha and her 8-month-old son lived with Martha's mother and stepfather. Martha's parents had divorced when she was 10, and her mother had married her stepfather 2 years ago, just 4 months before Martha learned that she was pregnant. Martha liked her new stepfather well enough, and they had developed a workable, if not really close, relationship during the first year. They worked on crossword puzzles together, and her stepfather enjoyed and appreciated Martha's artwork.

Martha said that after her baby was born, her stepfather became critical and demanding of her, especially about the ways that she took care of the baby. He seemed to love the baby and would spend time feeding and playing with him in the evenings, but he and Martha grew distant. Martha knew that her mother was bothered by the chill between her husband and her daughter, but no one seemed able to change things. As Martha talked about this at the relationship session of Taking Charge, she acknowledged that she was sensitive to her stepfather's criticism and reacted by shutting him out and behaving as if he were not even present most of the time. She also recognized that she appreciated her stepfather and wanted to restore the goodwill between them. She identified improving their relationship as her goal, and gave herself the task of talking with him to clear the air. This is Martha's description of her accomplished task:

What Happened to My First Task

I (did) X (did not) __ get this task accomplished this week. This is what happened:

My mom got sick, so she was asleep a lot on Sunday. I made lunch for me and my stepdad, and I told him about school and things while we ate. We didn't talk about serious stuff, but we made a get-well card for my mom. My stepdad and I are closer again, at least for now. We had fun.

My evidence that I completed this task is:

My mom (who signed the task validation) heard us laughing and kept her get-well card.

This is what I plan to do next:

Keep talking to my stepdad, even when he gets critical.

Focus Groups

We conducted focus groups for leaders and for participants at the conclusion of Studies 1 and 2. The purpose of these groups was to provide a clearer perception of the group experience for leaders as well as for teen mothers. Seven leaders participated in the focus group following Study 1, as well as seven in the leader group after Study 2.

These comments were recorded in leader focus groups:

- "I noticed the depth of sharing that was stimulated from doing specific tasks each week and returning to talk about them with the group... I liked seeing the girls' confidence grow from doing their tasks—how they began to take ownership of their own goals."

- "Having members set their own goals instead of having pre-determined goals set for them was different, and effective... kept them coming back.... When they 'caught on' they loved it."

- "Breaking the problem-solving down into small pieces made it manageable for the members—taught them how to look at their problems in a new way. Some in my group were amazed."

- "The problem-solving worksheet and other handouts were helpful to the girls and to us... structure and concrete tools to work with."

- "The topics were right-on—the girls related to all of them, especially the relationship one.... Could see they all had meaning to the members."

- "Appreciated the structure of working from a treatment manual... flexible but dependable.... I knew clearly what we were doing at every session—it adapted well to different cognitive levels of group members."

- "Liked that lunch and little gifts were built in—that meant a lot to the girls, especially in the beginning... made them feel special that 'outsiders' were jealous."

- "The point system was a big motivator—this helped in the beginning, and when they got going on their goals most of them didn't think about those things (incentives) as much."

- "The tasks! They made such a difference for the girls in my group who did them. They're crucial. Actually accomplishing things they never thought they would or could gave some of the girls a sense of control —something new for them."

These comments were recorded in participant focus groups:

- "I liked hearing the other girls' opinions about how they did things and what we all had in common. . . . All our interacting was good. I found out we're not alone. . . . I liked being able to speak freely about what's going on in my life and realizing that others have the same problems I do."

- "I loved the goals and working on them with everyone else. I wish we could have met more than once a week. I felt so at-home in the group."

- "Achieving my tasks was good for me. Since being in the group I've accomplished more little goals than I knew I could. That makes me feel better about everything in my life."

- "My leaders helped me a lot. I was pretty sure at first that I couldn't do the goals and tasks, but then gradually I did. Now I talk to my fiancé about goals because my leaders helped me learn to do that."

- "I learned how to set my goals and go for it by putting it on paper. I never would have thought before of putting it on paper. Now I will, and my boyfriend and I are both putting our priorities and goals on paper regarding us and our baby. I'm really thankful I did the group—I wasn't going to."

- "The group showed me how to focus on one thing and get it done without letting other things get in the way. Going step by step helped me learn how to get stuff done."

- "The relationship goal was my most important. I didn't get along with my fiancé's mom. That was a big goal I worked on, and at first I thought it backfired. But then after she got mad when I talked to her, she has started treating me different, more re-spectful, than before. So I think it worked in spite of everything."

- "I liked the school goal best, because some amazing things hap-pened after I did my tasks, especially with my teachers. My grades have definitely improved, and I speak up in class all the time now."

- "I wish we could have more sessions. This has helped me so much, but it seems like I just got into it and now it's over."

- "We needed more time in our sessions. There was a lot of writing to do, and we really needed more time just to talk to one another."

- "I liked having lunch during group. When we first started meeting and didn't know one another very well, eating lunch helped me loosen up and get to know the others easier. But I wish we could have had more pizza [laughter]."

Summary

The Taking Charge group curriculum was constructed with the best evidenced-based research that we could find on adolescent motherhood. Outcome research on the Taking Charge group curriculum is ongoing. In this chapter, we summarized the three clinical studies that have been completed on the Taking Charge group curriculum. These studies have included a total of 139 young mothers who were pregnant and parenting students in three regular high schools, three alternative schools, and one dropout recovery program. Study 1 ($n = 73$) and Study 2 ($n = 46$) included multiple treatment groups, whereas Study 3 ($n = 19$) was done with one treatment group. This chapter also discussed the results from qualitative data collected from Taking Charge participants that provide a wealth of information on the mothers' experiences and the impact of different aspects of the Taking Charge group curriculum. Several case studies were presented that illustrate this data.

Chapter 7

Presenting the Taking Charge Group at Your School

School-based clinical studies on the Taking Charge group tell us that it is an effective intervention with adolescent mothers. Results indicate that it helps adolescent mothers with social problem-solving and coping skills that serve them well in achieving academically and functioning more optimally in personal relationships, career building, and in their roles as parents. But the question that may be going through the minds of every school professional is, how well will Taking Charge work in my school? How adaptable is the Taking Charge group curriculum? In this final chapter, we explore the issues of adaptation in an easy question-and-answer format and share the practice wisdom that we have learned in our clinical experiences as we have offered the Taking Charge group curriculum in the real world of public schools. This chapter answers the top 10 questions that were asked by school professionals using Taking Charge in public schools.

How Do I Implement This Group at My School?

This is the ultimate question for educators, social workers, and other professionals working with teen parents. Anyone who works in a school setting knows that there are many things to consider when selecting and implementing social service and mental health programs—resources, political climate, administration priorities, and staff support, to name a few. In this chapter, we provide information and suggestions for that process by answering the 10 most frequently asked questions (FAQ) that we have often heard from teen parent staff in schools and at conferences where we have presented the curriculum.

Ten Most Frequently Asked Questions (FAQ) About the Taking Charge Curriculum

1. *What are the most persuasive arguments that I can give for having the Taking Charge group in my school?*

In addition to the relatively light demands that Taking Charge places on school time, facilities, and financial resources, these specifics have had strong positive response from principals and district administrators with previous studies:

- Taking Charge is demonstrated to support academic achievement for adolescent mothers. In the largest clinical study of the group, the group of young women who participated in the Taking Charge curriculum gained an *8-point advantage in their GPA* during the semester over an equivalent group who did not participate in the group. The Taking Charge participant group also *increased in school attendance from 79% to 91%*, whereas the nonparticipants made no gains in attendance.

- The curriculum can help expand staff resources. It can be led by volunteers, such as student interns, thus providing the intervention without adding to current staff loads. Because the curriculum is compatible with the professional training of school counselors and social workers, these and other mental health staff need only minimal training and time to supervise volunteer leaders or to facilitate the group.

2. *Can we really count on a volunteer to effectively lead the group?*

The structure and exceptional detail of the practice manual (chapter 3) make it feasible for a volunteer with some degree of experience and training to lead the Taking Charge group curriculum. The curriculum was specifically designed so that any mental health professional or experienced volunteer in the school can serve as a leader. The program has been led effectively by social work students (undergraduate as well as graduate), counselors, special education teachers, school nurses, and school social workers, and even one experienced, older teen parent. In the first clinical trial, the group was successfully cofacilitated by volunteer young adult mothers.

3. *In my school, teachers have the last word about when and what their students do during the school day. How can I gain their support and co-operation?*

It has been our experience that when teachers' own schedules and priorities are considered and when they are well informed about the group, most are supportive and some even appreciative of the Taking Charge group curriculum. In one instance, we were even able to get the Taking Charge group curriculum approved as an elective class once teachers understood the curriculum. The few exceptions to this have occurred when group leaders were unable to meet with teachers to explain goals and activities previous to beginning the group, resulting in irritation when participants were late to class after sessions. We have also found it helpful to assure teachers that the group will require no extra work for them, except to sign homework and extra credit verification for group participants. In more than a few instances, teachers have made positive comments to participants and leaders as they began to recognize increased interest in homework and class performance from group members. These four points may be most important in gaining and keeping teacher support:

- Meet with participants' teachers individually in advance of beginning the Taking Charge group, to explain your goals and activities. Give each a printed schedule of group days and times.

- Make it a priority to end sessions on time to prevent participants from being late to their class after group session. This clearly demonstrates your respect for the teacher's agenda and needs. Ask for the teacher's patience if this is unavoidable once or twice.

- When anything related to the group may affect a student's attendance or participation in class, inform the teachers of this well in advance.

- Do not ask teachers to keep extra records, make extra observations, or meet extra times with you or anyone else due to the group.

4. *What does it actually cost to present the group?*

The average cost is $15 to $20 per participant for incentives, in addition to minimal program supplies such as paper and folders. In previous Taking Charge studies, lunch or snacks were provided by participants or the school, and occasionally donated by local restaurants and businesses. The total cost of an 8-week group with 10 participants should be no more than $200.

5. The mental health budget in my district is tight. Where can I get help from other sources to help with the group?

Past leaders report that a surprising number of businesses and food establishments in the community are willing to contribute incentives items such as pizza coupons and movie passes. Businesses are more likely to give a positive response when these three conditions are met:

- They are well-informed about the group and how donations will be used.

- They are approached several weeks in advance.

- They are given control of when, what, and how much they contribute.

The same is true for contributions of food, such as pizza and hamburgers. Eating establishments, as well as stores and other businesses, are more likely to contribute if managers are given all the dates of the group and can pick the times and items they would like to donate. Taking Charge leaders in a small community were surprised, for example, after they explained the group to a local discount store manager in asking for a food donation that they could use for snacks. Two weeks later, the store presented them with six tins of cookies, along with eight $10 gift certificates to use for awards.

6. If we can't find funds to provide cash or gift certificates as awards for the point system, what else could we do?

With careful planning and cooperation from your school, awards can be created using the resources of the school or community that do not involve an outlay of cash. For example, participants who earned the highest award at one alternative high school were treated, with their babies, to a field trip to the city zoo. They were provided with school bus transportation and picnic lunches packed by the school cafeteria. At another school, leaders arranged for award recipients to receive manicures and hairstyles at a local school of cosmetology. In both these examples, group participants received the alternative "award" enthusiastically.

7. Can we use the Taking Charge curriculum with our young fathers?

Although Taking Charge has not yet been studied with young fathers, research reveals that adolescent fathers have need of virtually the same life skills and may be unprepared for the responsibility of parenthood in the same areas as adolescent mothers. Regardless of gender, adolescents face similar developmental tasks—establishing meaningful relationships, choosing a career, and developing a productive identity separate from their family of origin. Because we have not tested the curriculum with young men, we cannot assume that it would be as effective as with young women. However, similarities in developmental needs and societal expectations for young mothers and young fathers suggest that Taking Charge may be effective with young fathers. We will be including studies of the intervention with young fathers in our next phase of clinical study.

8. What if I need to reduce the group to six sessions?

We have tested Taking Charge only in the eight-session format, so we cannot speak with certainty to its effectiveness in a shorter format. However, when scheduling requires that it be reduced to six sessions, these components and activities should be included in order to retain the treatment integrity of the curriculum:

- *Session 1:* Help participants understand the purpose and goals of the group. Establish group rules, especially around confidentiality. Begin to tally points at the end of this session, and stay current with each subsequent session.

- *Session 2:* Teach the problem-solving process, and guide participants through the process with their education goal and task identification. Distribute a small attendance incentive to participants at the end of the session.

- *Sessions 3, 4, and 5:* Begin each session with a review and discussion of task experiences from the prior week. Devote the remainder of each session to one of the remaining three life area goals and task identification. Distribute a small attendance incentive at the end of Session 5.

- *Session 6:* Review and discuss task experiences from the prior week. Review the entire group experience and discuss how things learned can be carried beyond the group. Announce point totals at the end of this session.

9. Do I need to be concerned about HIPAA policy regarding privacy in using this curriculum?

As a mental health intervention, the Taking Charge group may be circumscribed by the same HIPAA regulations as other health-related services in your school. Although HIPAA policy is uniform across the country, local interpretation and HIPAA-related procedures vary among school districts. Usually someone in each school district's administrative staff serves as HIPAA officer for the district. One step in planning for the Taking Charge group should be to meet with your school's or district's HIPAA representative. Be prepared to make possible adjustments, especially in protecting the identity of group members and in maintaining and storing confidential records.

10. Do group leaders require special outside training?

To gain sufficient mastery of the Taking Charge group curriculum, we recommend that leaders read this book and spend a few hours reviewing and discussing the training manual in chapter 3 in some detail, perhaps with another practitioner or supervisor. Past leaders of the group report that they needed to work through the problem-solving process several times with real problems of their own before they felt prepared to help group participants with that process.

The degree of leaders' previous training and experience, of course, should determine the extent of training. For example, those with little experience in mental health counseling, leading groups, or working with adolescents may need a review cognitive-behavioral theories, group dynamics, or adolescent behavioral dynamics before moving on to the Taking Charge group curriculum. It is always advantageous to receive training in a workshop or in-service from an expert on Taking Charge and build in some additional supervision and consultation on your leadership skills, as was pointed out in chapter 4.

Note: As discussed, the Taking Charge group is designed to be facilitated by social workers, counselors, teachers, and other school-based practitioners, as well as by student interns and experienced volunteers under the supervision of a school professional. When additional guidance or training is required for introducing the curriculum into the school program, the authors or their designees are often available to provide consultation or training in the same format provided by previous leaders.

Summary

In this final chapter, we explored the issues of adaptation in an easy question-and-answer format and shared the practice wisdom that we have gained as we have offered the Taking Charge group curriculum in the real world of public schools. School-based clinical studies on the Taking Charge group tell us that it is an effective intervention with adolescent mothers. This chapter answered the top 10 questions that we have been asked by school professionals who were using or considering the Taking Charge group at their schools. These questions concerned marketing, cooperating with teachers, flexibility of sessions, school policies, resources, and training issues. The Taking charge group curriculum appears to be highly adaptable to most public school settings.

References

Aloise-Young, P. A., & Chavez, E. L. (2002). Not all school dropouts are the same: Ethnic differences in the relation between reason for leaving school and adolescent substance use. *Psychology in the Schools, 39*(5), 539–548.

Bandura, A. (1986). The explanatory and predictive scope of self-efficacy. *Journal of Social and Clinical Psychology, 4*, 359–373.

Bandura, A. (1991a). Self-efficacy mechanism in physiological activation and health-promoting behavior. In J. Madden IV (Ed.), *Neurobiology of learning, emotion and affect* (pp. 229–269). New York: Raven.

Bandura, A. (1991b). Social cognitive therapy of self-regulation. *Organizational Behavior and Human Decision Processes, 50*, 248–287.

Bandura, A. (1992). Exercise of personal agency through the self-efficacy mechanism. In R. Schwarzer (Ed.), *Self efficacy: Thought control of action* (pp. 3–38). Washington, DC: Hemisphere.

Bandura, A. (1995). Modeling. In A. S. R. Manstead & M. Hewstone (Eds.), *Blackwell encyclopedia of social psychology* (pp. 409–411). Oxford: Blackwell.

Bandura, A. (1999). Social cognitive theory of personality. In D. Cervone & Y. Shoda (Eds.), *The coherence of personality*. New York: Guilford Press.

Bandura, A. (2003). Role of affective self-regulatory efficacy in diverse spheres of psychosocial functioning. *Child Development, 74*(3), 769–782.

Bandura, A. (2004). Health promotion by social cognitive means. *Health Education and Behavior, 31*(2), 143–163.

Barth, R. P., & Schinke, S. P. (1984). Coping with daily strain among pregnant and parenting adolescents. *Journal of Social Service Research, 7*, 51–63.

Beauvais, F., Chavez, E. L., & Oetting, E. R. (1996). Drug use, violence, and victimization among White American, Mexican American, and American Indian dropouts, students with academic problems, and students in good academic standing. *Journal of Counseling Psychology, 43*(3), 292–299.

Belcazar, H., Peterson, G., & Krull, J. L. (1997). Acculturation and family cohesiveness in Mexican American pregnant women: Social and health implications. *Family Community Health, 20*, 16–31.

Benn, R., & Saltz, E. (1989). The effect of grandmother support on teen parenting and infant attachment patterns within the family. In *Teen mothers: Their fathers, their mothers, their boyfriends, and their babies.* Symposium conducted at the biennial meeting of the Society for Research in Child Development, Kansas City.

Berg, I. K., & Shilts, L. (2005). *Classroom solutions: Woww approach.* Milwaukee: Brief Family Therapy Center.

Berndt, T. J., & Savin-Williams, R. C. (1996). Variations in friendships and peer-group relationships in adolescence. In P. Tolan & B. Cohler (Eds.), *Handbook of clinical research and practice with adolescents.* New York: Wiley.

Betz, N. E., & Hackett, G. (1981). The relationship of career-related self-efficacy expectation to perceived career options in college women and men. *Journal of Counseling Psychology, 28,* 399–410.

Biddle, B. J. (1979). *Role theory: Concepts and research.* Huntington, NY: Krieger.

Black, C., & DeBlassie, E. R. (1985). Adolescent pregnancy: Contributing factors: Consequences, treatment, and plausible solutions. *Adolescence, 20,* 281–290.

Black, D. R. (1987). A minimal intervention program and a problem-solving program for weight control. *Cognitive Therapy and Research, 11,* 104–120.

Bloom, B. L. (1992). *Planned short-term psychotherapy.* Boston: Allyn & Bacon.

Bogat, G. A., Caldwell, R. A., Guzman, B., Galasso, L., & Davidson, W. S. H. (1998). Structure and stability of maternal support among pregnant and parenting adolescents. *Journal of Community Psychology, 26*(6), 549–568.

Boothroyd, R., Gomez, A., & Armstrong, M. (2005). Young and poor: The well-being of adolescent girls living in families receiving Temporary Assistance for Needy Families Program. *Journal of Child and Family Studies, 14*(1), 141–154.

Botvin, G. J., & Botvin, E. M. (1992). Adolescent tobacco, alcohol, and drug abuse: Prevention strategies, empirical findings, and assessment issues. *Developmental and Behavioral Pediatrics, 12,* 290–301.

Bunting, L., & McAuley, C. (2004). Research review: Teenage pregnancy and motherhood: The contribution of support. *Child and Family Social Work, 9,* 207–215.

Center for Health and Healthcare in Schools. (2007). School-based health centers—background. Retrieved March 28, 2007, from http://www.healthinschools.org/sbhcs/sbhc.asp.

Chase-Lansdale, P. L., Brooks-Gunn, J., & Paikoff, R. L. (1992). Research and programs for adolescent mothers: Missing links and future promises. *American Behavioral Scientist, 35*(3), 290–312.

Chodorow, N. J. (1989). What is the relation between the psychoanalytic psychology of women and psychoanalytic feminism? *Annual of Psychoanalysis, 17,* 215–261.

Christmon, D. (1990). The unwed adolescent father's perception of his family and of himself as a father. *Child and Adolescent Social Work, 7*(4), 275–283.

Clemmens, D. (2003). Adolescent motherhood: A meta-analysis of qualitative studies. *American Journal of Maternal Child Nursing, 28*(2), 93–99.

Codega, S. A., Pasley, B. K., & Kreutzer, J. (1990). Coping behaviors of adolescent mothers: An exploratory study and comparison of Mexican-Americans and Anglos. *Journal of Adolescent Research, 5*(1), 34–53.

Colletta, N. D., & Gregg, C. H. (1981). Adolescent mothers' vulnerability to stress. *Journal of Nervous and Mental Disorders, 169*, 50–54.

Corcoran, J., Franklin, C., & Bennett, P. (2000). Ecological factors associated with adolescent pregnancy and parenting. *Social Work Research, 24*, 29–39.

Corcoran, M., Gordon, R., Laren, D., & Solon, G. (1992). The association between men's economic status and their family and community of origins. *Journal of Human Resources, 27*, 575–601.

Cormier, W. H., Otani, A., & Cormier, L. S. (1986). The effects of problem-solving training on two problem-solving tasks. *Cognitive Therapy and Research, 10*, 95–108.

Covington, D. L., Carl, J. C., Daley, J. G., Cushing, D., & Churchill, M. P. (1988). Effects of the North Carolina prematurity prevention program among public patients delivering at New Hanover Memorial Hospital. *American Journal of Public Health, 78*, 1493–1495.

Culp, R. E., Appelbaum, M. I., Osofsky, J. D., & Levy, J. A. (1989). Adolescent and older mothers: Comparison between prenatal maternal variables and newborn interaction measures. *Infant Behavior & Development, 11*(3), 353–362.

Davis, L. V. (1996). Role theory and social work treatment. In F. J. Turner, (Ed.), *Social work treatment: Interlocking theoretical approaches* (4th ed.). New York: Free Press.

Deal, L. W., & Holt, V. L. (1998). Young maternal age and depressive symptoms: Results from the 1988 National Maternal and Infant Health Survey. *American Journal of Public Health, 88*(2), 266–270.

de Anda, D. (1998). The evaluation of a stress management program for public school adolescents. *Child and Adolescent Social Work Journal, 15*(1), 73–85.

de Anda, D., & Becerra, R. M. (1984). Social networks for adolescent mothers. *Social Casework: The Journal of Contemporary Social Work, 65*, 172–181.

de Anda, D., Darroch, P., Davidson, M., Gilly, J., Javidi, M., Jefford, S., Komorowski, R., & Morejon-Schrobsdorf, A. (1992). Stress and coping among pregnant adolescents. *Journal of Adolescent Research, 7*(1), 94–109.

DeBolt, M. E., Pasley, B. K., & Kreutzer, J. (1990). Factors affecting the probability of school dropout: A study of pregnant and parenting adolescent females. *Journal of Adolescent Research, 5*(3), 190–205.

De Jong, P., & Berg, I. K. (2002). *Interviewing for solutions* (2nd ed.). Pacific Grove: Brooks/Cole.

Di Giovanni, L (2006). Substance abuse prevention: Effective school-based programs. In C. Franklin, M. B. Harris, & P. Allen-Meares (Eds.), *The school services sourcebook: A guide for school professionals.* New York: Oxford University Press.

Duncan, G., & Yeung, W. J. (1995). Extent and consequences of welfare dependence among America's children. *Children and Youth Services Review, 17,* 157–182.

Dupper, D. R. (1998). An alternative to suspension for middle school youths with behavior problems: Findings from a "school survival" group. *Research on Social Work Practice, 8*(3), 354–366.

D'Zurilla, T. J., & Nezu, A. M. (1982). Social problem-solving in adults. In P. C. Kendall (Ed.), *Advances in cognitive-behavioral research and therapy* (pp. 202–269). New York: Academic Press.

D'Zurilla, T. J., & Nezu, A. M. (1990). Development and preliminary evaluation of the social problem-solving inventory. *Psychological Assessment: A Journal of Consulting and Clinical Psychology, 78,* 104–126.

D'Zurilla, T. J., & Nezu, A. M. (1999). *Problem-solving therapy: A social competence approach to clinical intervention* (2nd ed.). New York: Springer.

D'Zurilla, T. J., & Sheedy, C. F. (1992). The relation between social problem-solving ability and subsequent level of academic competence in college students. *Cognitive Therapy and Research,* 16, 589–599.

Elson, M. (1986). *Self psychology in clinical social work.* New York: W. W. Norton.

Endler, N. S., & Parker, J. (1990). Multi dimensional assessment of coping: A critical review. *Journal of Personality and Social Psychology, 58,* 844–854.

Erickson, E. (1968). *Identity and the life cycle.* New York: W. W. Norton.

Forman, S. G., Linney, J. A., & Brondino, M. J. (1990). Effects of coping skills training on adolescents at risk for substance abuse. *Psychology of Addictive Behaviors, 4*(2), 67–76.

Forste, R., & Tienda, M. (1992). Race and ethnic variation in the schooling consequences of female adolescent sexual activity. *Social Science Quarterly, 73,* 12–30.

Fortune, A. E. (1985). *Task-centered practice with families and groups.* New York: Springer.

Franklin, C., Biever, J., Moore, K., Clemons, D., & Scamardo, M. (2001). The effectiveness of solution-focused therapy with children in a school setting. *Research on Social Work Practice, 11*(4), 411–434.

Franklin, C., & Corcoran, J. (1999). Preventing adolescent pregnancy: A review of programs and practices. *Social Work in Health Care, 45*(1), 40–52.

Franklin, C., Corcoran, J., & Harris, M. B. (2004). Risk and the protective factors for adolescent pregnancy: Basis for effective intervention. In M. W. Fraser (Ed.), *Risk and resilience in childhood: An ecological perspective*. Washington, DC: NASW Press.

Franklin, C., & Hopson, L. (2007, in press). Facilitating the use of evidence-based practice in community organizations. *Journal of Social Work Education*.

Franklin, C., Kim, J. S., & Tripodi, S. (2006). Solution-focused, brief therapy interventions for students at-risk to dropout. In C. Franklin, M. B. Harris, & P. Allen-Meares (Eds.), *The school services sourcebook* (pp. 691–704). New York: Oxford University Press.

Franklin, C., McNeil, J. A., & Wright, R. (1991). The effectiveness of social work in an alternative school for high school dropouts. *Social Work With Groups, 14*(2), 59–73.

Franklin, C., & Nurius, P. (1996). *Families in society*. Milwaukee: Families International, Inc.

Freud, S. (1953). Three essays on sexuality. *Standard Editions*, (Vol. 7, pp. 3–122). London: Hogarth. (Original work published 1905).

Garfield, S. L. (1994). Research on client variables in psychotherapy. In S. L. Garfield & A. E. Bergin (Eds.), *Handbook of psychotherapy and behavior change* (4th ed., pp. 192–204). New York: Wiley.

Garvin, C. (1986). Practice with task-centered groups. In A. Fortune (Ed.), *Task-centered practice with families and groups*. New York: Springer.

Gegas, V., & Seff, M. A. (1990). Families and adolescents: A review of the 1980s. *Journal of Marriage and the Family, 52*, 941–958.

Gitterman, A., & Shulman, L. (1994). *Mutual aid groups, vulnerable populations, and the life cycle*. New York: Columbia University Press.

Glodich, A., & Allen, J. G. (1998). Adolescents exposed to violence and abuse: A review of the group therapy literature with an emphasis on preventing trauma reenactment. *Journal of Child and Adolescent Group Therapy, 8*(3), 135–153.

Gottman, J. M. (1999). *The marriage clinic: A scientifically based marital therapy*. New York: W. W. Norton.

Gove, W. R. (1975). *The labelling of deviance: Evaluating a perspective*. Oxford, England: John Wiley & Sons.

Greene, R. (2006). *Social work practice: A risk and resilience perspective*. Pacific Grove, CA: Brooks/Cole.

Hallfors, D., Veves, J. L., Iritani, B., Cho, H., Khatapoush, S., & Saxe, L. (2002). Truancy, grade point average, and sexual activity: A meta-analysis of risk indicators for youth substance abuse. *Journal of School Health, 72*(5), 205–212.

Harris, M. B. (2006, in review). Quasi-experimental evaluation of a cognitive behavioral group for adolescent mothers. *Children & Schools.*

Harris, M. B., & Franklin, C. (2003). Effectiveness of a cognitive-behavioral group intervention with Mexican American adolescent mothers. *Social Work Research, 17*(2), 71–83.

Havinghurst, R. J. (1972). *Developmental tasks and education* (3rd ed.). New York: McKay.

Hayes, C. D. (1987). Consequences of adolescent childbearing. In C. D. Hayes (Ed.), *Risking the future: Adolescent sexuality, pregnancy and child bearing.* Washington, DC: National Academy Press.

Hayes, S. D., Follette, V. M., & Linehan, M. M. (2004). *Mindfulness and commitment therapy: Expanding the cognitive-behavioral tradition.* New York: Guilford Press.

Hogue, A., & Liddle, H. A. (1999). Family-based preventive intervention: An approach to preventing substance abuse and antisocial behavior. *American Journal of Orthopsychiatry, 69,* 275–293.

Hopson, L. (2006). Effective HIV prevention in schools. In C. Franklin, M. B. Harris, & P. Allen-Meares (Eds.), *The school services sourcebook* (pp. 289–295). New York: Oxford University Press.

Hunter, F. T., & Youniss, J. (1982). Changes in functions of three relations during adolescence. *Developmental Psychology, 18,* 806–811.

Jerusalem, M., & Mittag, W. (1995). Self-efficacy in stressful life transitions. In A. Bandura (Ed.), *Self-efficacy in changing societies* (pp. 177–201). New York: Cambridge University Press.

Kalil, A., Spencer, M. S., Spieker, S. J., & Gilchrist, L. D. (1998). Effects of grandmother coresidence and quality of family relationships on depressive symptoms in adolescent mothers. *Family Relations: Interdisciplinary Journal of Applied Family Studies, 47*(4), 433–441.

Kalil, A., Ziol-Guest, K. M., & Coley, R. L. (2005). Perceptions of father involvement patterns in teenage-mother families: Predictors and links to mothers' psychological adjustment. *Family Relations, 54*(2), 197–211.

Kann, L., Kinchen, S., Williams, B., Ross, J., Lowry, R., Hill, C., Grunbaum, J., Blumson, P., Collins, J., & Kolbe, L. (1998). Youth risk behavior surveillance—United States, 1997. *Morbidity and Mortality Weekly Report, 47*(SS-3), 1–89.

Kenemore, E., & Spira, M. (1996). Mothers and their adolescent daughters: Transitions and transformations. *Child and Adolescent Social Work Journal, 13*(3), 225–240.

Kissman, K. (1998). High risk behaviour among adolescent mothers. *International Journal of Adolescence & Youth, 7*(3), 179–191.

Klein, T. M. (1998). Adolescent pregnancy and loneliness. *Public Health Nursing, 15*(5), 338–347.

Koss, M. P., & Shiang, J. (2002). Research on brief psychotherapy. In A. E. Bergin & S. I. Garfield (Eds.), *Handbook of psychotherapy and behavior change* (5th ed., pp. 665–700). New York: Wiley.

Koss-Chioino, J., & Vargas, L. (1999). *Working with Latino youth: Culture, development, and context.* San Francisco: Jossey-Bass.

Kral, R. (1995). *Strategies that work: Techniques for solutions in schools.* Milwaukee: Brief Family Therapy Press.

Kymissis, P. (1993). Group psychotherapy with adolescents. In H. Kaplan & B. Sadock (Eds.), *Comprehensive group psychotherapy* (3rd ed., pp. 577–584). Baltimore: Williams & Wilkins.

Lazarus, R. S., & Folkman, S. (1984). *Stress, appraisal and coping.* New York: Springer.

Lazarus, R. S., & Launier, R. (1978). Stress-related transactions between person and environment. In L. Pervin & M. Lewis (Eds.), *Perspectives in international psychology* (pp. 287–327). New York: Plenum.

Lear, J. (2006). Best practice for designing and developing school-based health centers. In C. Franklin, M. B. Harris, & P. Allen-Meares (Eds.), *The school services sourcebook* (pp. 1003–1010). New York: Oxford University Press.

Leitenberg, H., & Saltzman, H. (2000). A statewide survey of age at first intercourse for adolescent females and age of their male partners: Relation to other risk behaviors and statutory rape implications. *Archives of Sexual Behavior, 29*(3), 203–215.

Lent, R. W., Brown, S. D., & Larkin, K. C. (1987). Comparison of three theoretically derived variables in predicting career and academic behaviors: Self-efficacy, interest congruence, and consequence thinking. *Journal of Counseling Psychology, 34,* 293–298.

Levy, S. R., Perhats, C., Nash-Johnson, M., & Welter, J. F. (1992). Reducing the risks in pregnant teens who are very young and those with mild mental retardation. *Mental Retardation, 30*(4), 195–203.

Locke, E. A., & Latham, G. P. (1990). *A theory of goal setting and task performance.* Englewood Cliffs, NJ: Prentice-Hall.

Luster, T., & Small, S. (1997). Sexual abuse history and number of sex partners among female adolescents. *Family Planning Perspectives, 29,* 204–211.

MacNair, R. R., & Elliott, T. R. (1992). Self-perceived problem-solving ability, stress, appraisal, and coping over time. *Journal of Research in Personality, 26,* 399–413.

Mahoney, M. J. (2003). *Constructive psychotherapy: A practical guide.* New York: Guilford.

Marques, R. P., & McKnight, A. J. (1991). Drug abuse risk among pregnant adolescents attending public health clinics. *American Journal of Drug & Alcohol Abuse, 17*(4), 399–413.

Martin, C. A., Hill, K. K., & Welch, R. (1998). Adolescent pregnancy, a stressful life event: Cause and consequence. In T. Miller (Ed.), *Children of trauma: Stressful life events and their effects on children and adolescents.* Madison, CT: International Universities Press.

Mattaini, M. (2006). Creating a violence-free school climate/culture. In C. Franklin, M. B. Harris, & P. Allen-Meares (Eds.), *The school services sourcebook.* New York: Oxford University Press.

Mayer, G. R., Mitchell, L. K., Clementi, T., & Clement-Robertson, E. (1993). A dropout prevention program for at-risk high school students: Emphasizing consulting to promote positive classroom climates. *Education and Treatment of Children, 16*(2), 135–146.

McWhirter, B. T., & Page, G. L. (1999). Effects of anger management and goal setting group interventions on state-trait anger and self-efficacy beliefs among high risk adolescents. *Current Psychology: Developmental, Learning, Personality, Social, 18*(2), 223–237.

Metcalf, L. (1995). *Counseling toward solutions: A practical solution-focused program for working with students, teachers, and parents.* San Francisco: Jossey-Bass.

Miller, D. B. (1994). Influences on parental involvement of African American adolescent fathers. *Child and Adolescent Social Work, 11*(5), 363–378.

Moore, P., & Terrett, C. (1998). Highlights of the 1996 National Youth Gang Survey. *OJJDP fact sheet (#86).* Washington, DC: Office of Juvenile Justice and Delinquency Prevention.

Mott, F. L. (1986). The pace of repeated childbearing among young American mothers. *Family Planning Perspectives, 18*(1), 5–12.

Mott, F. L., & Marsiglio, W. (1985). Early childbearing and completion of high school. *Family Planning Perspectives, 17*(5), 234–237.

Murphy, J. (1996). Solution-focused brief therapy in the school. In S. Miller, M. Hubble, & B. Duncah (Eds.), *Handbook of solution-focused brief therapy* (pp. 184–204). San Francisco: Jossey-Bass.

Nadelman, A. (1994). Sharing the hurt: Adolescents in a residential setting. In A. Gitterman & L. Shulman (Eds.), *Mutual aid groups, vulnerable populations, and the life cycle* (2nd ed., pp. 163–181). New York: Columbia University Press.

National At-Risk Education Network. (2006). Who is at-risk? Retrieved July 12, 2006, from http://www.atriskeducation.net.

Nezu, A. (1985). Differences in psychological distress between effective and ineffective problem solvers. *Journal of Counseling Psychology, 32*, 135–138.

Nitz, K., Ketterlinus, R. D., & Brandt, L. J. (1995). The role of stress, social support and family environment in adolescent mothers' parenting. *Journal of Adolescent Research, 10,* 358–382.

Opuni, K. A., Smith, P. B., Arvey, H., & Solomon, C. (1994). The Northeast Adolescent Project: A collaborative effort to address teen-age pregnancy in Houston, Texas. *Journal of School Health, 64*(5), 212–215.

Panzarine, S. (1986). Stressors, coping, and social supports of adolescent mothers. *Journal of Adolescent Health Care, 7,* 153–161.

Parke, R., & Collmer, M. (1975). Child abuse: An interdisciplinary analysis. In M. Hetherington (Ed.), *Review of child development research* (Vol. 5). Chicago: University of Chicago Press.

Paskiewicz, L. (2001). Pregnant adolescents and their mothers. *American Journal of Maternal Child Nursing, 26*(1), 33–38.

Passino, A. W., Whitman, T. L., Borkowski, J. G., Schellenbach, C. J., Mazwell, S. E., & Keogh, D. R. E. (1993). Personal adjustment during pregnancy and adolescent parenting. *Adolescence, 28*(109), 97–123.

Patterson, J., & McCubbin, H. (1991). A-COPE: Adolescent-coping orientation for problem experiences. In H. I. McCubbin, A. I. Thompson, & M. A. McCubbin (Eds.), *Family assessment: Resiliency, coping and adaptation: Inventory's research and practice.* Madison: University of Wisconsin.

Pearson, L. C., & Banerji, M. (1993, Spring). Effects of a ninth-grade dropout prevention program on student academic achievement, school attendance, and dropout rate. *Journal of Experimental Education, 61,* 247–256.

Perkins, D. F., Luster, T., Villarreal, F. A., & Small, S. (1998). An ecological, risk-factor examination of adolescents' sexual activity in three ethnic groups. *Journal of Marriage and the Family, 60,* 660–673.

Pierce, G. R., Saranson, B. R., Saranson, I. G., Joseph, H. J., & Henderson, C. A. (1996). Conceptualizing and assessing social support in the context of the family. In G. R. Pierce, B. R. Saranson, & I. G. Saranson (Eds.), *Handbook of social support and the family* (pp. 3–23). New York: Plenum.

Pinderhughes, E. B. (1988). Significance of culture and power in the human behavior curriculum. In C. Jacobs & D. D. Bowles (Eds.), *Ethnicity and race: Critical concepts in social work* (pp. 152–166). Silver Spring, MD: National Association of Social Workers.

Pines, D. (1988). Adolescent pregnancy and motherhood: A psychoanalytical perspective. *Psychoanalytic Inquiry, 8*(2), 234–251.

Raj, A., Silverman, J. G., & Amaro, H. (2000). The relationship between sexual abuse and sexual risk among high school students: Findings from the 1997 Massachusetts Youth Risk Behavior Survey. *Maternal and Child Health Journal, 4*(2), 125–134.

Reid, W. J. (1996). Task-centered social work. In F. J. Turner (Ed.), *Social work treatment: Interlocking theoretical approaches* (4th ed., pp. 617–640). New York: Free Press.

Reid, W. J., & Epstein, L. (1972). *Task-centered casework.* New York: Columbia University Press.

Reid, W. J., & Fortune, A. E. (2006). Task-centered practice: An exemplar of evidence-based practice. In A. R. Roberts and K. R. Yeager (Eds.), *Foundations of evidence-based social work practice* (pp. 194–203). New York: Oxford University Press.

Reid, W. J., & Fortune, R. (2002). *The task planner.* New York: Columbia University Press.

Resnick, M. D., Chambliss, S. A., & Blum, R. W. (1993). Health and risk behaviors of urban adolescent males involved in pregnancy. *Families in Society: The Journal of Contemporary Human Services, 74,* 366–374.

Rhein, L. M., Ginsburgh, K. R., Schwarz, D. F., Pinto-Martin, J. A., Zhao, H., Morgan, A. P., & Slap, G. B. (1997). Teen father participation in child rearing: Family perspectives. *Journal of Adolescent Health, 21,* 244–252.

Rice, K. G., & Meyer, A. L. (1994). Preventing depression among young adolescents: Preliminary process results of a psycho-educational intervention program. *Journal of Counseling & Development, 73,* 145–152.

Richardson, R. A., Barbour, N. E., & Bubenzer, D. L. (1995). Peer relationships as a source of support for adolescent mothers. *Journal of Adolescent Research, 10*(2), 278–290.

Richman, J. M., Rosenfeld, L. B., & Bowen, G. L. (1998). Social support for adolescents at risk of school failure. *Social Work, 43,* 309–323.

Roberts, A. R., & Yeager, K. R. (2005). Lethality assessments and crisis intervention with persons presenting with suicidal ideation. In A. R. Roberts (Ed.), *Crisis intervention handbook: Assessment, treatment, and research* (3rd ed., pp. 35–63). New York: Oxford University Press.

Robins, C. J., Schmidt, H., & Linehan, M. M. (2004). Dialectical behavior therapy: Synthesizing radical acceptance with skillful means. In *Mindfulness and commitment therapy: Expanding the cognitive-behavioral tradition* (pp. 30–44). New York: Guilford.

Roosa, M. (1986). Adolescent mothers, school drop-outs, and school-based intervention programs. *Family Relations: Interdisciplinary Journal of Applied Family Studies, 35,* 313–317.

Rumberger, R. W. (1987). High school dropouts: A review of the issues and evidence. *Review of Educational Research, 57,* 101–121.

Sandfort, J. R., & Hill, M. S. (1996). Assisting young unmarried mothers to become self-sufficient. The effects of different types of early economic support. *Journal of Marriage and the Family, 58*(2), 311–326.

Savin-Williams, R., & Berndt, T. J. (1990). Friendship and peer relations. In S. Feldman & G. R. Elliott (Eds.), *At the threshold: The developing adolescent* (pp. 277–307). Cambridge, MA: Harvard University Press.

Seitz, V., & Apfel, N. H. (1993). Adolescent mothers and repeated childbearing: Effects of a school-based intervention program. *American Journal of Orthopsychiatry, 63,* 572–581.

Seitz, V., & Apfel, N. H. (1999). Effective interventions for adolescent mothers. *Clinical Psychology Science and Practice, 6*(1), 50–66.

Silver, W. S., Mitchell, T. R., & Gist, M. E. (1995). Responses to successful and unsuccessful performance: The moderating effect of self-efficacy on the relationship between performance and attributions. *Organizational Behavioral and Human Decision Processes, 62,* 286–299.

Sklare, G. (1997). *Brief counseling that works: A solution-focused approach for school counselors.* Thousand Oaks, CA: Corwin Press/Sage.

Stern, M., & Alvarez, A. (1992). Pregnant and parenting adolescents: A comparative analysis of coping response and psychosocial adjustment. *Journal of Adolescent Research, 7*(4), 469–493.

Stern, M., & Zevon, M. A. (1990). Stress, coping, and family environment: The adolescents' response to naturally occurring stressors. *Journal of Adolescent Research, 5,* 290–305.

Stevens-Simon, C., & Nelligan, D. (1998). Strategies for identifying and treating adolescents at risk for maltreating their children. *Aggressive & Violent Behavior, 3*(2), 197–217.

Stevens-Simon, C., O'Connor, P., & Bassford, K. (1994). Incentives enhance postpartum compliance among adolescent prenatal patients. *Pediatrics, 93,* 737–743.

Stock, J. L., Bell, M. A., Boyer, D. K., & Connell, F. A. (1997). Adolescent pregnancy and sexual risk-taking among sexually abused girls. *Family Planning Perspectives, 29*(4), 200–203, 227.

Thornberry, T., & Burch, J. (1997). Gang members and delinquent behavior. *OJJDP Juvenile Justice Bulletin.* Washington, DC: Office of Juvenile Justice and Delinquency Prevention.

Tolor, A., & Fehon, D. (1987). Coping with stress: A study of male adolescents' coping strategies to adjustment. *Journal of Adolescent Research, 2,* 33–42.

Trad, P. V. (1994). Adolescent pregnancy: An intervention challenge. *Child Psychiatry & Human Development, 24*(2), 99–113.

Turner, R. J., Grindstaff, C. F., & Phillips, N. (1990). Social support and outcome in teenage pregnancy. *Journal of Health and Social Behavior, 31,* 43–57.

Unger, D. G., & Wandersman, L. P. (1988). The relation of family and partner support to the adjustment of adolescent mothers. *Child Development, 59,* 1056–1060.

Uno, D., Florsheim, P., & Uchino, B. N. (1998). Psychosocial mechanisms underlying quality of parenting among Mexican-American and White adolescent mothers. *Journal of Youth and Adolescence, 27*(5), 585–605.

U.S. Department of Health and Human Services. (1999). Children and mental health. In *Mental health: A report of the surgeon general—executive summary* (chap. 3). Retrieved July 1, 2006, from http://www.surgeongeneral.gov/library/mentalhealth/chapter3/sec1.html.

Ward, M. J., Carlson, E., Plunkett, S. W., & Kessler, D. B. (1998). Adolescent mother-infant attachment: Interactions, relationships, and adolescent development. In *Adolescents as mothers: Family processes and child outcomes.* Symposium conducted at the biennial of the Society for Research on Adolescence, Alexandria, VA.

Wasserman, G. A., Brunelli, S. A., & Rauh, V. A. (1990). Social supports and living arrangements of adolescent and adult mothers. *Journal of Adolescent Research, 5*(1), 54–66.

Webb, W. H. (1999). *Solutioning: Solution-focused interventions for counselors.* Philadelphia: Accelerated Press.

Wege, J. W., & Moller, A. T. (1995). Effectiveness of a problem-solving training program. *Psychological Reports, 76,* 507–514.

Williams, C., & Vine, W. (1999). Broken past, fragile future: Personal stories of high-risk adolescent mothers. *Journal of the Society of Pediatric Nurses, 4*(1), 15–23.

Yalum, I. D. (1995). *The theory and practice of group psychotherapy.* New York: Basic Books.

Zeidner, M., & Hammer, A. L. (1990). Life events and coping resources as predictors of stress symptoms in adolescents. *Personality and Individual Differences, 11,* 693–703.

Zimmerman, B. J., & Martinez-Pons, M. (1990). Student differences in self-regulated learning. *Journal of Educational Psychology, 82,* 51–59.

Zuravin, S. J., & DiBlasio, F. A. (1996). The correlates of child physical abuse and neglect by adolescent mothers. *Journal of Family Violence, 11*(2), 149–166.

Index

career. *See* employment/career
challenges
  and adolescent motherhood, 4, 8,
    11, 54
  of career, 103
  and coping efforts, 51, 55
  of education, 87–89, 93
  life's, 4, 8, 11, 39
  of social problem-solving, 80,
    81–82
  and solution-focused therapy,
    39–40
change, 36, 47, 48, 53, 54–55, 61
child abuse, 17, 21–22
child care, 4, 167–68, 170, 171
child neglect, 17, 21–22
clinics, 19
cognitive-behavioral theory,
    44–45, 54
cognitive flexibility, 53
cognitive organization, 33
coleadership, 127–28
Community Service Society of
    New York, 60
competence, 70
compromise, 133
confidence, 3
confidentiality, 129
Confidentiality Agreement, 77, 112
contraception, 12, 19
control, 47
coping
  action-focused, 51
  active, 53, 69
  in adolescence, 52
  anticipatory, 51
  emotion-focused, 51, 59
  in life domains, 5
  method, 52
  passive, 52, 55, 69
  problem-focused, 11, 49, 51, 52,
    54–56, 67, 69–71
  skills, 3, 11, 24, 31, 44, 55, 61, 185
  with stress, 32
  task-focused behavior, 59
  transactional coping theory, 45,
    50–52

culturally competent leadership,
    141–51
culturally relevant group rituals,
    147–48
cultural metaphors/icons, 145
cultural values, 142–45
customs, 150

decision making, 57
depression, 10, 14
deShazer, Steve, 37
despondency, 50
developmental tasks, 33–34, 189
dichos, 149
direct actions, 51
documentation, 136–37
domain, definition of, 5
donations, 188
dreams, 41, 80, 81–82, 84, 85
dropouts, 8–13, 165–66
drug abuse, 12–13, 19

economics, 26–28
education
  academic achievement, 8, 68,
    164–65, 166–70, 186
  and career, 85
  as challenge, 87–89, 93
  dropouts, 8–13, 165–66
  exercise, 85–88
  goal, 90–95
  high school graduation, 6, 8,
    26, 68
  as life domain, 3, 5–13, 15, 29,
    31, 56
  as life dream, 84
  Taking Charge curriculum for, 25
efficacy. *See* self-efficacy
efficacy theory, 32, 48, 70
emotional state, 50, 55
emotion-focused coping, 51, 69
employment/career
  case examples, 176–77
  and education, 85
  goals and tasks, 101–4, 173–77

as life domain, 3, 5, 23–29, 31, 34, 56
    as life dream, 85
English language, 149
environment, 47
experiences, 4, 5, 7, 41, 49

failure, 48–49
family
    life, 34, 144
    problem solving, 158
    relationships, 14–16
    roles, 142–44
    values, 145
fatherhood, 16–17, 189
financial support, 17
flexibility, 53
focus groups, 180–83
food, 132, 148, 150, 151, 188
friendship, 13, 16, 58
future, 61

games, 151
gangs, 11
gifts, 133, 150
goal(s)
    directed tasks, 57
    education, 90–95, 166–70
    employment/career, 101–4, 173–77
    as guides through emotional issues, 50
    parenting, 85, 99–101, 170–73
    personal relationship, 84, 95–99, 173, 178–80
    self-selected, 64, 70
    setting, 32, 37–42, 48, 49, 57
    of Taking Charge curriculum, 67–69
    well-constructed, 68
    worksheet, 115
Gottman, John, 53
grade point average (GPA), 12, 160, 164, 186
grades. See academic achievement

graduation, 6, 8, 26, 68
grandmothers, 14, 15, 171
group process, 129–32
    disengagement stage, 131–32
    initial stage, 129–30
    transition stage, 130
    working stage, 131
group rituals, 147–48
group traditions, 150–51

harm, 51
health, 18–20
high school graduation, 6, 8, 26, 68
HIPAA policy, 190
HIV/AIDS, 11
homework/extra credit verification sheet, 119–20
homicide, 11
human agency, 46
human development, 33
humor, 150

icons, 145
immigrants, 141, 145–46, 150
incentives, 3, 46, 132–33, 187–88
income, 27, 28
independence, 144, 145
interpersonal roles, 34
intervention fidelity, 137–38, 139

job. See employment/career

knowledge, 27

language, 43–44, 145–46, 149
Latinos, 150
leadership
    coleadership, 127–28
    culturally competent, 141–51
    focus groups, 180–81
    intervention fidelity, 137–38
    of outcome studies, 159–60

prenatal care, 18, 19
present time, 61
privacy, 190
problem
  definition of, 56, 57
  solution to, 81
  specification, 61–62
problem-focused coping, 11,
    49, 51, 52, 54–56, 67,
    69–71
problem-solving
  of adolescents, 55, 133, 134
  in education, 91
  family, 158
  radical acceptance strategies, 53
  in relationships, 98
  skills, 55, 56–58, 134
  and solution-building, 42–44
  strengthening, 31
  of Taking Charge curriculum, 79,
    80–83
  and task-centered model, 61
  theory, 45
  See also social problem-solving
progress notes sheet, 124

quality of life, 23

radical acceptance strategies, 53,
    54, 55
records, 136–37
recreational customs, 150
reinforcement, 3
relationships. *See* personal
    relationships
repetition, 135–36
resilience, 36, 40, 48
rewards, 46–47, 77–78, 113,
    132–33, 188
rites of passage, 147
rituals, 147–48
role conflict, 34–35
role discontinuity, 34–35
role expectations, 34
role functioning, 34

role norms, 34
role-playing, 63

school achievement. *See* academic
    achievement
school attendance, 163–64, 167–68,
    169–70, 186
school violence, 11
selected environment, 47
self-awareness, 55
self-control, 47
self-efficacy, 32, 47–50, 55, 56,
    59, 70
self-regulatory capability, 46
self-reliance, 158
self-sufficiency, 52
  across life domains, 31, 33–34
  in context of cultural roles,
    144–45
  and social problem-solving skills,
    56, 57, 58
  through employment/career, 23,
    25–26
  through school achievement, 6, 7,
    68
separation, 145
sexual abuse, 10–11
sexual activity, 4, 12, 13
single parenthood, 21
skills training programs, 45
social cognitive theory, 58
social isolation, 8, 10
social learning programs, 45
social learning theory, 32, 44–47, 48
social models, 49
social persuasion, 49–50, 59
social problem-solving, 3, 185
  active, 50
  competent use of, 67
  measures of, 158
  process, 32, 80–83, 133–36, 138
  skills, 24, 31, 44, 56–58, 59,
    69–70
Social Problem-Solving Inventory–
    Revised, Short Form (SPSI-R),
    158, 160, 162–63

social roles, 34
social support, 158
solutions, 40, 42–44, 56, 57, 81
Spanglish, 149
Spanish language, 149
SPSI-R. *See* Social Problem-Solving
    Inventory–Revised, Short Form
staffing report sheet, 125
stereotypes, 150
strengths-based approach, 36, 43
stress, 14, 32, 34–35, 48, 50, 69
subgroups, 128–29
substance abuse. *See* drug abuse
success, 48
suicide, 11
surprise gifts, 133

Taking Charge group curriculum
    change-focused approach, 54
    Confidentiality Agreement, 77, 112
    developmental framework, 32,
        33–35
    duration and times of, 71–72
    ending group, 106–9, 131–32
    extending group, 109
    forms and handouts, 110–25
    frequently asked questions about,
        186–90
    getting started, 73–76, 111
    goals, 25–26, 31, 67–69
    group expectations and rules, 76–77
    group modality, 58–59, 72–73
    group process, 129–32
    and life domains, 3–8, 10–13,
        15–17, 19–20, 22–29, 31
    major theoretical components, 32
    outcome studies, 153–83
    planning of, 71–73
    points system and awards, 77–78,
        113, 121–23, 132–33, 136–37,
        188
    practice training manual, 67–125,
        190

problem-solving process, 79,
    80–83
in school setting, 26, 31, 64, 65,
    71, 185–91
self-sufficiency as goal of,
    25–26, 31
sessions 1 to 6, 189–90
sessions 1 to 8, 73–109
solution-focused brief therapy
    framework, 36–42
structure and modality, 58–59
subgroups, 128–29
task-centered group model, 32,
    59–64, 65
See also leadership
TANF. *See* Temporary Aid to Needy
    Families
task-centered group model, 32,
    59–64, 65
task-centered objectives, 70–71
task worksheets, 116–18
teachable moments, 64
teachers, 187
teenagers. *See* adolescents
Temporary Aid to Needy Families
    (TANF), 6
testimonies, 49
threat, 51, 55
traditions, 150–51
transactional coping theory, 45,
    50–52, 56
transitions, 48
triadic reciprocal causation, 46
trust, 129, 130

vicarious experiences, 49
volunteers, 186

weapons, 11
welfare, 6
women, 144, 150
work. *See* employment/career